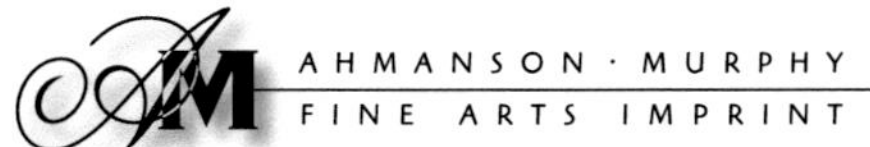

THE AHMANSON FOUNDATION

has endowed this imprint
to honor the memory of

FRANKLIN D. MURPHY

who for half a century
served arts and letters,
beauty and learning, in
equal measure by shaping
with a brilliant devotion
those institutions upon
which they rely.

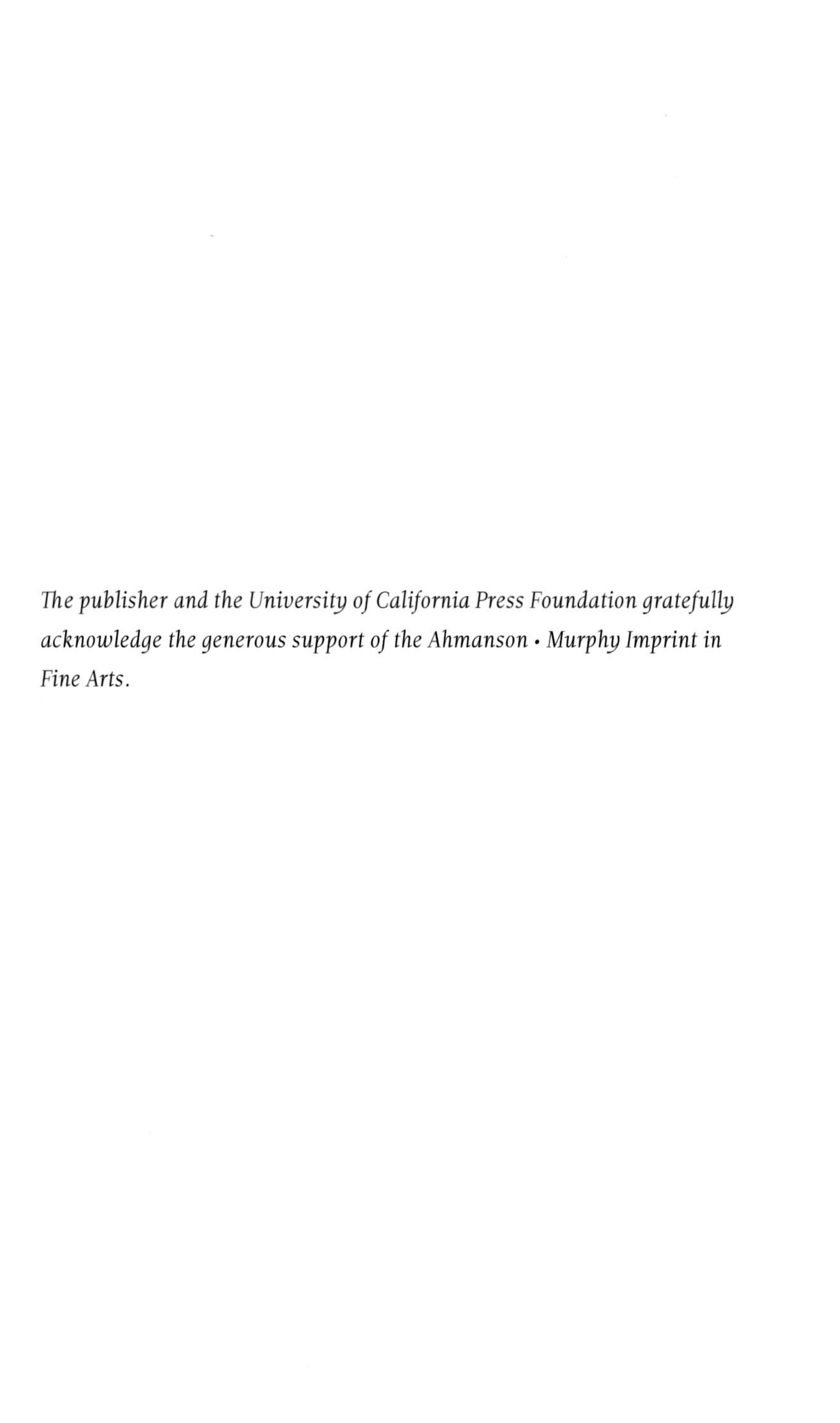

The publisher and the University of California Press Foundation gratefully acknowledge the generous support of the Ahmanson • Murphy Imprint in Fine Arts.

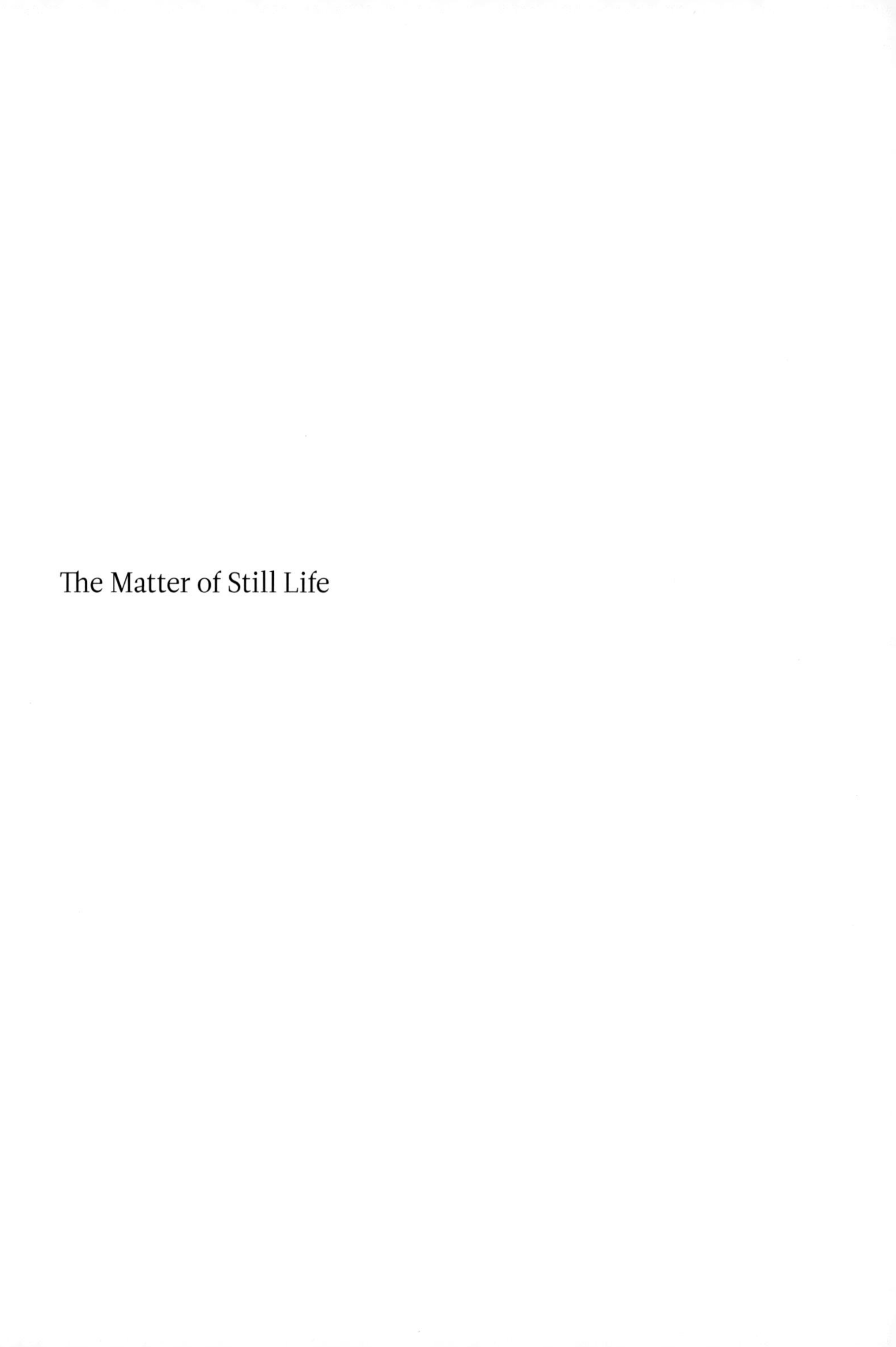

The Matter of Still Life

THE FRANKLIN D. MURPHY LECTURE SERIES

David Cateforis, Series Editor (2014–)

Established in 1979 through the Kansas University Endowment Association in honor of former chancellor Dr. Franklin D. Murphy, the Murphy Lectureship in Art brings distinguished art historians, critics, and artists to the University of Kansas, where they participate in the teaching of a graduate seminar in the Kress Foundation Department of Art History and deliver two public lectures, one at the Spencer Museum of Art and one at the Nelson-Atkins Museum of Art. Those lectures serve as the basis for the books in this series.

THE FRANKLIN D. MURPHY LECTURERS IN ART

1979	Pierre Rosenberg
1980	Brian O'Doherty
1981	Xia Nai
1982	Richard Field
1983	Robert G. Calkins
1983	Svetlana Alpers
1984	Nobuo Tsuji
1986	David Rosand
1987	James Cahill
1987	William Vaughan
1988	Walter S. Gibson
1989	Thomas Lawton
1990	Johei Sasaki
1992	Marilyn Aronberg Lavin and Irving Lavin
1994	Lothar Ledderose
1994	John Szarkowski
1996	Karal Ann Marling
1996	John M. Rosenfield
1998	Serafin Moralejo
1999	Helmut Brinker
2001	Yi Sŏng-mi
2001	Wanda M. Corn
2003	Donald McCallum
2004	Roberta Smith
2005	Tamar Garb
2007	Okwui Enwezor
2008	David M. Lubin
2009	Christopher M. S. Johns
2010	Toshio Watanabe
2012	Michael Brenson
2014	Cynthia Hahn
2017	Christine M. E. Guth
2018	Erika Doss
2020	Carol Armstrong
2021	Paul Binski
2022	Alfreda Murck
2022	Karl Kusserow
2024	Peter Sturman

The Matter of Still Life

Between Chardin and Morandi

CAROL ARMSTRONG

UNIVERSITY OF CALIFORNIA PRESS

in association with the Spencer Museum of Art and Kress Foundation Department of Art History, the University of Kansas

The publisher gratefully acknowledges the generous contributions to this book provided by the University of Kansas Provost's Office and the Franklin D. Murphy Lecture Fund through the Spencer Museum of Art and the Kress Foundation Department of Art History, the University of Kansas.

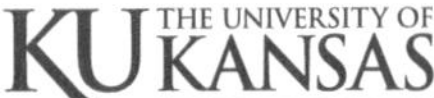

University of California Press
Oakland, California

Library of Congress Cataloging-in-Publication Data

Names: Armstrong, Carol M., author.

Title: The matter of still life : between Chardin and Morandi / Carol Armstrong.

Other titles: University of Kansas Franklin D. Murphy lecture series.

Description: Oakland, California : University of California Press, in association with the Spencer Museum of Art and Kress Foundation Department of Art History, the University of Kansas, [2026] | Series: The Franklin D. Murphy Lecture Series | Includes bibliographical references and index.

Identifiers: LCCN 2025044772 | ISBN 9780520416994 (cloth)

Subjects: LCSH: Chardin, Jean Baptiste Siméon, 1699–1779—Criticism and interpretation. | Morandi, Giorgio, 1890–1964—Criticism and interpretation. | Still-life painting.

Classification: LCC ND1390 .A83 2026

LC record available at https://lccn.loc.gov/2025044772

Manufactured in the United States of America

GPSR Authorized Representative: Easy Access System Europe, Mustamäe tee 50, 10621 Tallinn, Estonia, gpsr.requests@easproject.com

35 34 33 32 31 30 29 28 27 26
10 9 8 7 6 5 4 3 2 1

CONTENTS

PREFACE

The two essays in this book, which were originally delivered as lectures in the fall of 2020 as part of the Franklin D. Murphy Lectureship in the Kress Foundation Department of Art History at the University of Kansas, concern two different figures from two different moments in the history of still-life painting: the eighteenth-century French artist Jean-Baptiste-Siméon Chardin and the twentieth-century Italian painter Giorgio Morandi.[1] United in their lifelong dedication to the lowest of genres on the old academic hierarchy of subject matter, the works of these two artists from different places in Europe are separated by two centuries, while the essays that address them pursue divergent tacks.

The first of the two essays digs into the particular historical moment in which Chardin worked, addressing not only Chardin's still-life paintings themselves but also the several ways of writing about paintings and material objects found in the *Salons* authored by his contemporary, the philosophe Denis Diderot, as well as in some of the essays and illustrations that made up the famous multivolume *Encyclopédie* that Diderot directed in the mid-eighteenth century, placing both within an extended history of descriptive or "ekphrastic" writing. The lengthier second essay, by contrast, takes a more expansive view of still-life painting, setting Morandi's obsession with the genre against its longer European history, on the one hand, and in relation to the roughly contemporaneous variation on the theory of object relations developed by the English psychoanalyst Donald Winnicott, on the other hand. Thus while the two essays are in some senses similarly bifurcated, they also diverge substantially in their approaches to "the matter of still life."

Yet at the same time, each of the essays radiates outward from a close reading of a single still-life painting, taken as a centerpiece, in which I perform my own ekphrastic exercise of trying to render the visual experience of still-life painting in words in such a way as to blur the boundary between description and interpretation. This long-standing practice of mine goes as far back as the first art history papers that I wrote as a student—and it happens that the first seminar paper I ever wrote concerned the genre of still life, focusing as it did on an in-depth comparison of two flower paintings, one by Willem van Aelst, of the Dutch seventeenth century, and the other by Vincent van Gogh. For me it is now a settled belief that attentive description *is* interpretation, at least when informed by critical thinking and theorization.[2]

Of course the question arises, Why still life? Why describe, why write about still life in particular? That is a question that each of the two essays in this book attempts to answer performatively, and as such I shall return to it in a moment. But it is also a question that animated a project that I first undertook in 2012: namely, a self-published, genre-crossing book called *Still Lives* that combined a short story with five short art historical set pieces, as well as prose poems and my own still-life photographs. *Still Lives*, which, in addition to its focus on still life, was also an experiment in different modes of writing and imaging, contained the germ of this present volume, and indeed substantial portions of its second essay, on "Giorgio Morandi and the Matter of Still Life," began life in that project.[3]

So, let me pick up the threads, here, of the argument I initially tried to make in *Still Lives*, concerning the three interlinked themes that tie together the two essays in this book: the question of still life as a genre, the problematics of descriptive writing, and the concept of "material thought," underwritten as it is by the "material turn" that has marked the discipline of art history in recent decades. On the first question—why still life per se?—the genre has long attracted me, perhaps perversely, precisely because of its lowliness, its unpretentiousness and sometimes its quietly radical resistance to the loftiest registers of the humanist tradition. It is, I would argue, a profoundly democratic genre that invites a kind of loving, slowed-down attention to the humble, the marginalized, and the overlooked, to that which has been demoted and treated with contempt, but also to those small things and apparently insignificant details that seem to defy verbal exposition.[4] Indeed, in the absence of narrative alibis, most of the time, for its devotion to material objects, it is a genre that instead solicits a kind of wordless wonder at the mysterious otherness of the object world, along with the tricks of illusionism used to render that world, the seductive materialities of both paintings and the things they depict, and those things' intransigence in the face of the human subject that would encompass and possess them, the human eye that would grasp them, that would but cannot devour them. Even, or perhaps especially, when they are inventories of possessions in an early mercantile economy, as many seventeenth-century Dutch still lifes purported to be.[5]

Which brings me to the problem of descriptive writing, whose fancy name is "ekphrasis."[6] To try to write in detail about still life is perhaps another futile way of trying to incorporate its wordless obscurities, but if so, I find that I am quite interested in that futility. Fascinated from the outset by the relationship between the visual and the verbal, particularly within the history of art-critical writing in its different forms (which for me encompass ekphrastic poetry and the artist novel as well as *Salons* and exhibition reviews), I have also long understood that the one does not and cannot reduce to or be adequately translated into the other, and that the best writing about art is that which acknowledges and wrestles with that fact. Indeed that was part of the appeal, for me, of the capacious, multidisciplinary field that we know as art history, and that caused me to choose that field, rather than literary history, as my own: namely, that the challenge of writing about visual art lies partly in the incommensurability of the literary and the artifactual, and in the pushback that the materiality of the visual artwork offers to a verbal intelligence. This is nowhere more true than in still life, which has from its inception been regarded as the most abjectly materialist of all the genres in its status as a material thing representing other material things, and which I argue represents a form of "material thought" about itself in relation to the worldly goods that it renders.

And so I come to the idea of "material thought," and the "material turn" in art history. Some of the strands of that "material turn" are not mine. For instance, I am not a historian, an ethnographer, or an anthropologist of material culture, whether local or global; rather, I am pretty staunchly attached to depictive objects (mostly in the European tradition) made for the sole purpose of being contemplated, rather than to serve other, more practical functions like cooking, drinking, and eating, clothing and adorning the body, and/or furnishing the home.[7] Neither am I much of a devotee of "thing theory," with its invocations of the active agency of apparently inanimate things, though I have learned much from such approaches and their undermining of the subject-object binaries of the Western philosophical tradition.[8] But I am a believer in a phenomenological notion of "material thought," which proposes that pictorial artists *think* with and in the materials that they use, and in relation to the material world that they represent.[9] According to that notion, the materiality, facture, composition, and subject matter of a work of visual art are all mutually imbricated, effectively undermining the mind-versus-matter, humanities-versus-crafts, invention-versus-skill dichotomies that underwrite such things as the hierarchy of genres, the high status of literary subjects, and the low status of still life in that hierarchy. Thus, when I write about a humble ceramic coffeepot and a simple glass of water, or gessoed bottles, cardboard boxes, and flea-market tins, as painted by Chardin and Morandi, respectively, it is less to contextualize them as commodities circulating within their local social worlds or their global marketplaces than to try to make their materiality matter as a form of thought. And if I have succeeded, hopefully it is in some sense by acknowledging the aporia, even the failure, built into the enterprise.

I give this preface's last word to Edmund de Waal, writing about four of my favorite artists, Chardin and Morandi, as well as Paul Cézanne and the poet Rainer Maria Rilke:

> To catch that fugitive apprehension and make it slow into the fullness of Chardin's glass of water (three cloves of garlic and a brown jug), Cézanne's apples, Morandi, will take a lifetime, but as Rilke wrote, "you must change your life." And he should know. He wrote poems, *Ding Gedichte*, that were still lives too.[10]

To slow down and take a close look at things normally taken for granted, and then to try to write that slowed-down looking: it has indeed taken much of a lifetime. And yes—to twist Rilke's words just slightly, but to embrace entirely the spirit in which they were uttered—to do so has been quietly, constantly life-changing all along the way. The two essays in this volume are but two pieces of that constancy.

CHAPTER ONE

Chardin, Diderot, and the Muteness of Made Things

Between Ekphrasis and the Encyclopedia

I begin and end with a single still life: the *Glass of Water and Coffee Pot* painted by Jean-Baptiste-Siméon Chardin in 1760, whose diminutive size accords with its modesty of conception (figure 1). In an essay appearing in a 2016 issue of the UK online journal *Independent*, the arts writer Tom Lubbock discovered a kinship between this little painting and the following lines from a poem by Bertolt Brecht: "'Of all works I prefer / Those used and worn / Copper vessels with dents and flattened rims / Knives and forks whose wooden handles / Many hands have grooved: such shapes / Seem the noblest to me.'"[1] The *Glass of Water and Coffee Pot* contains no "copper vessels with dents and flattened rims," no "knives and forks whose wooden handles" have been "grooved" by "many hands," though many of Chardin's still lifes *did* include such things: copper pots abound in the first period of his work especially, in his kitchen still lifes, and projecting knives—a staple of the still-life tradition since the seventeenth century—are to be found all the way through, from the beginning to the end of his career. Nonetheless, I agree that the little painting matches the spirit of Brecht's lines: the designation of the humblest of things as also the "noblest" of things, the human aspect of the everyday, the sense of the timeworn and the much used, and the

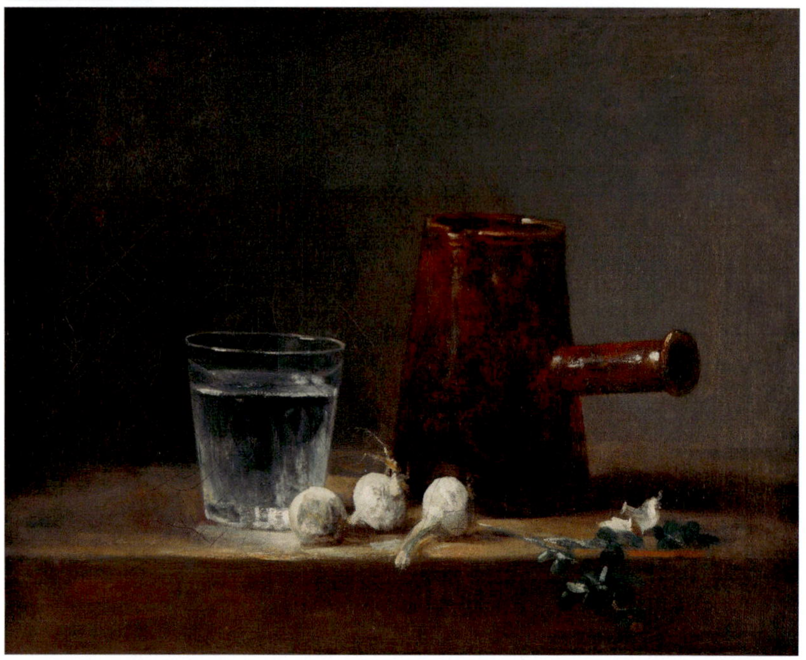

Figure 1. Jean-Baptiste-Siméon Chardin, *Glass of Water and Coffee Pot*, 1760. Oil on canvas. 12 × 16 in. (32 × 41.3 cm). Carnegie Museum of Art, Pittsburgh.

tactile appeal of, in this case, a single stemless glass of water with the hint of fluting at its base, but no other special shaping to its flaring cylinder; the inverted, truncated cone of a brown-glazed earthenware coffeepot whose hollow handle seems to offer itself to the grasping hand (while also defeating that hand in its quest to curl its fingers around that handle); three small bulbs of garlic and one stray white blossom that have little to do with the drinking of water or coffee; all casting shadows on a bare ledge that might or might not be stone, against a nondescript background, possibly the vertical plane of a wall, whose intersection with the horizontal top of the ledge is only hinted at.

Or maybe it is circulating air, just barely distinguished from the solid substance of the surface on which the two little vessels are seen to sit. For, though there is no steam issuing from the coffeepot—as there was, sometimes, from teapots and coffee cups elsewhere in Chardin's still-life and genre paintings—there *is* a sense of the slightest of contrasts, not only between the glinting transparency of one vessel and the opacity and dull shine of the other, or between the different, gravity-bound, shadow-casting weightinesses of the two vessels, whose shapes mimic and invert each other, versus the relative lightness of the garlic bulbs and blossom, but also among the solid, the liquid, and the airy. There are the different hollow solidities of glass and ceramic versus the solid stoniness of the ledge; there is the liquidity of the water that fills the glass (the painting gives us no clue as to whether the coffeepot is full or empty or half full/half empty); and there is the airiness of the void around them, which, with the hints of light on the respective rims of the pair of vessels and on the handle of the coffeepot, suggests some sort of atmosphere that circulates around and in between the things that inhabit it—and inhabit it they do. For habitation is evoked, even without the suggestions of human consumption that run rife through the longer history of still-life painting: the glass and the coffeepot are like a mute but individuated pair who *live* in the space this painting provides for them.

And all of this by dint of a manner of painting that shows off the painter's touch on the surface of the canvas and his ability to confect substances as different as hard glass, hardy fired clay with its dim gleams of glaze, the papery outer skins of garlic bulbs, and the slight petals of the broken-stemmed blossom out of the same paint material, and even the same restricted palette of whites, browns, and greens. And despite the fact that the perspectival ellipses of the tops of the glass and the coffeepot hardly seem to provide enough room for the volumes they are meant to indicate, nor the handle of the coffeepot to project enough to be handled. This is a still life, then, that suggests a deep relationship between the tactile crafting of painting and the equally tactile crafting and using of the determinedly quotidian, unremarkable objects and materialities that it depicts with such quiet—and quietly radical—dignity. Silent they sit there, awaiting not so much our bodily use as our perception—optical sensation hovering just on the threshold of tactile apprehension—and our contemplation.

+ + + +

This essay addresses the intersection between the preoccupations of two eighteenth-century Frenchmen as they touch on the matter of still life: our painter Chardin and the Enlightenment philosopher Denis Diderot. Both men came from artisanal families: Chardin was the son of a carpenter/cabinetmaker who specialized in billiard tables, and Diderot was the child of a cutler/knife maker. Chardin's artisanal background would come to the foreground, quite literally, in his two specialties as a painter: still life, which preoccupied him throughout his career, from his acceptance into the Royal Academy in 1728 until 1768 or so, when his eyesight began to decline, and genre painting, usually with still-life objects in the front plane of the picture, which he took up in the 1730s, in order to address the challenge of figure painting, with its higher ranking in the academic hierarchy of genres. For his part, Diderot's artisanal family background was registered in the unusual respect he paid to the French crafts and craft trades, and to the intricacy and mechanics of different kinds of workmanship, in the massive enterprise that he directed, for a while with his colleague, the physical scientist and mathematician Jean le Rond d'Alembert, until Diderot took over sole editorial responsibility for it in 1759: namely, the twenty-eight-volume set of the *Encyclopédie*, or, in English, the *Encyclopedia: The Reasoned Dictionary of the Sciences, Arts and Métiers, by a Society of Men of Letters,* published between 1751 and 1772, with the last eleven of those volumes dedicated to the over three thousand illustrational plates that comprised the *Encyclopedia*'s visual component. Diderot was responsible for about seven hundred of the articles written for the *Encyclopedia*, including the long entry on "Encyclopédie" that defined the project as the complete "enchainement de conoissances," or a totalized, cross-referenced compendium of human knowledge.[2]

But Chardin's and Diderot's paths intersected most directly in the annual Salons, in which Chardin actively participated between 1737, when they resumed after an interregnum hiatus, and his death in 1779, serving successfully as counselor, treasurer, and secretary, and beginning in 1761, as the overseer of the hanging of the Salon. From 1759 to 1781, Diderot wrote *Salons*—written reviews of the contents of these royally sponsored exhibitions—for the small, select readership of the *Correspondance Littéraire* published by the German-born Friedrich Melchior Baron von Grimm: these *Salons* were without illustrations, and were addressed to a European elite of royals and aristocrats, philosophers and men and women of letters who were unlikely to have gone to the Salons themselves, and therefore had not seen the works addressed, though they may have been familiar with similar pieces, particularly as they circulated in the form of engravings after the original works. In that context, Diderot often singled out Chardin as one of his favorite painters, in spite of the fact that he himself was much more inclined toward the so-called "nobler" genres that were based in the human figure and the literary imagination: history and genre painting. Paradoxically, however, Diderot was critical of Chardin's figure painting and preferred the painter's still-life efforts.[3]

Diderot's brand of art criticism was exemplified in the long rumination about Louis Michel Van Loo's portrait of him in a dressing gown and notably without his wig (figure 2), when it appeared in the Salon of 1767: several pages of playfully chatty musings that depart from the portrait in order to talk about how Diderot wanted to think of himself and how he would have preferred to have been depicted, in which those imaginings effectively substituted for the portrait itself—which probably would not have been seen by the readers of Grimm's *Correspondance Littéraire*.[4] More famously, in Diderot's much longer treatment of seven works in the same Salon by the landscape painter Claude-Joseph Vernet, he went to town with this fanciful mode of writing: some eighty pages of dialogue with an imaginary interlocutor, in which Diderot imagined himself walking from scene to scene—indeed, Diderot dubbed the first six of Vernet's paintings "sites," only to switch back to the designation of "picture" for the seventh of them, finally acknowledging that his imaginary wandering through Nature was actually a peregrination through the Salon. In the case of the Vernet paintings, in short, the literary production of landscapes effectively substituted for the painted landscapes that were the ostensible subject of Diderot's contemplation, at once signposting the verbal production of landscape imagery in the mind of the reader, and gesturing to the mimetic mode of the painted landscapes, a mode that seems to solicit just the kind of back-and-forth between Nature and Art that Diderot built into his discussion of those paintings.[5]

But if not the lengthiest, the most elaborate of such verbal fantasies were written two years earlier, for the Salon of 1765, in the face of two figural paintings: a sentimental genre picture, *Girl with a Dead Bird*, by another of Diderot's favorite painters, Jean-Baptiste Greuze (figure 3); and a history painting by Jean-Honoré Fragonard, *Coresus Sacrificing Himself to Save Callirhoe* (figure 4). For Greuze's painting, Diderot developed a highly amusing, if slightly embarrassing, three-page fictional conversation with the girl herself, in the process of which he described the painting lingeringly, in caressive detail. But that description presents itself as a conjuring, not of the *painting* but of the girl that the painting represents, and it is put to the service of a fantasy of an eroticized encounter, teasingly paternalistic in tone, between the barely pubescent girl and the fifty-four-year-old roué—the "old flirt," as Diderot would describe himself in his review of the Van Loo portrait two years later. Once more, the mimetic mode of the painting is signaled in the oscillation between the picture and its referent, as is the substitution of the literary for the pictorial rendering of the girl, in the *reader's*

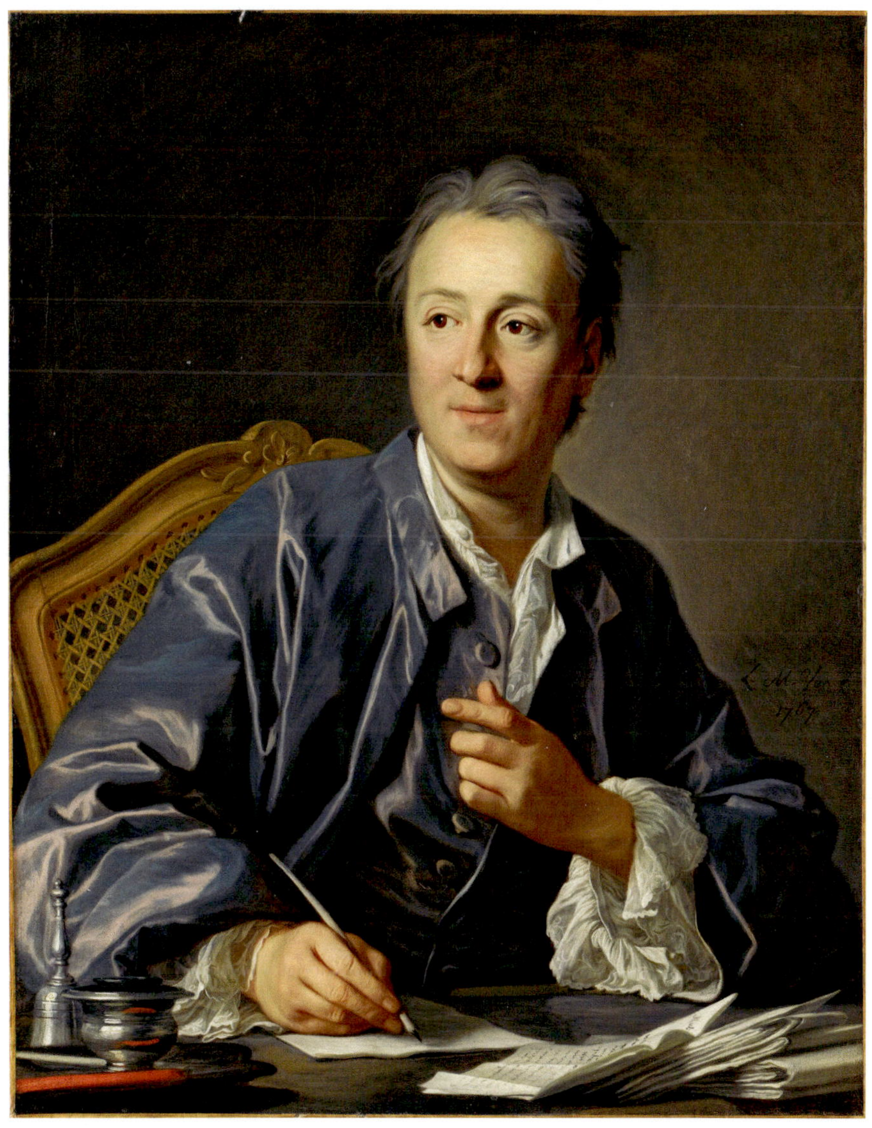

Figure 2. L. M. Van Loo, *Portrait of Denis Diderot*, 1767. Oil on canvas. 32 × 26 in. (81 × 65 cm). Louvre.

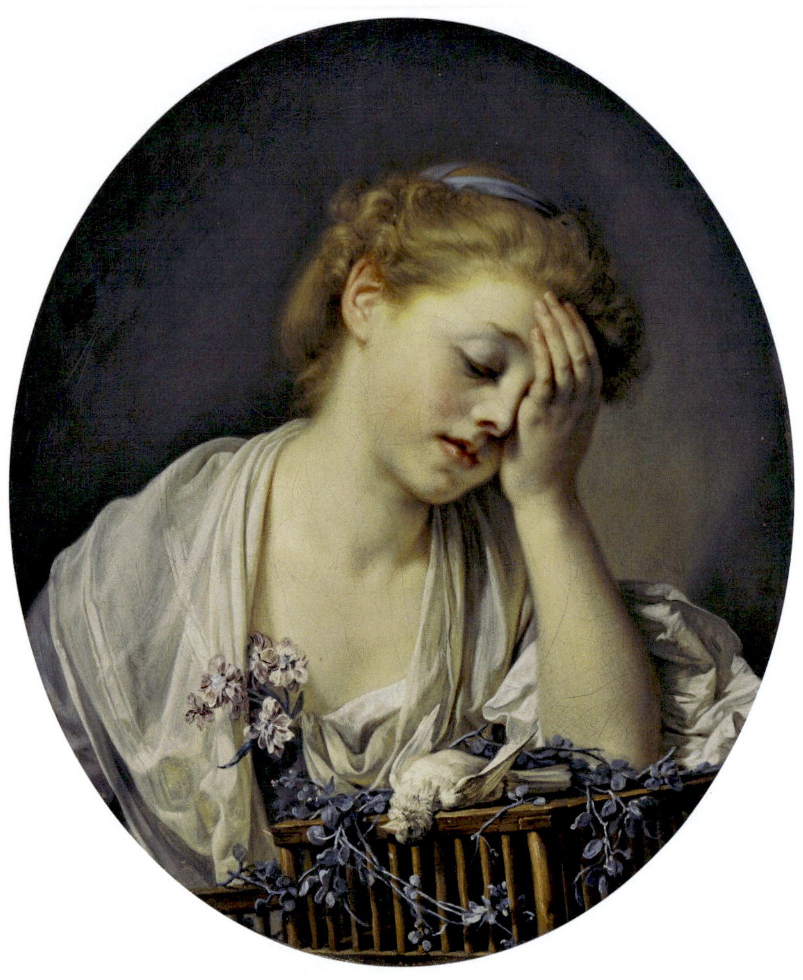

Figure 3. J. B. Greuze, *Girl with a Dead Bird*, 1765. Oil on canvas. 21 × 18 1/8 in. (53.3 × 46 cm). National Galleries of Scotland, Edinburgh. Bequest of Lady Murray of Henderland 1861.

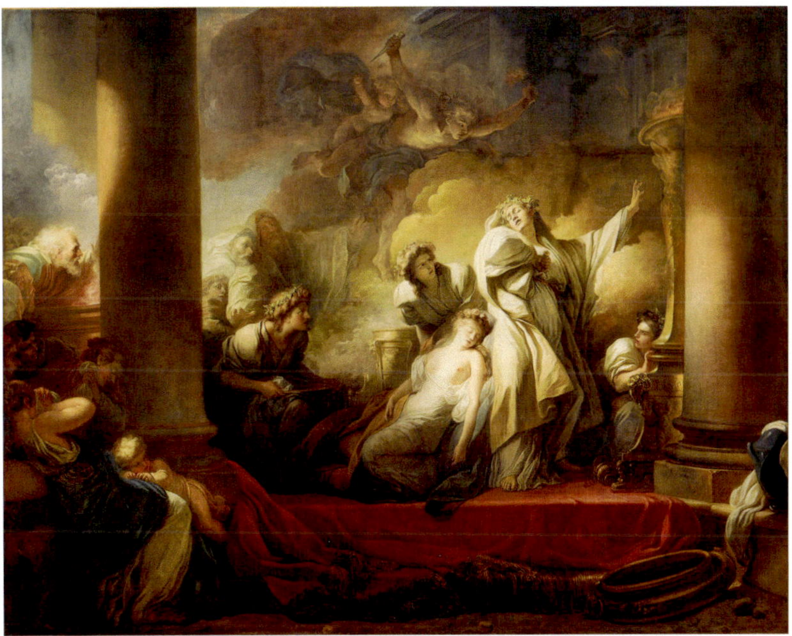

Figure 4. J.H. Fragonard, *Coresus Sacrificing Himself to Save Callirhoe*, 1765. Oil on canvas. 129 × 160 in. (309 × 400 cm). Louvre. © RMN-Grand Palais / Art Resource, NY.

(rather than the viewer's) imagination: again, taking into account the fact that the audience of the *Correspondance Littéraire* was made up of readers more than of viewers.[6]

As for Fragonard's rather strange effort at a history painting, Diderot devoted six pages to a protocinematic dreamscape based on the trope of Plato's cave, in which prisoners chained inside a dark cavern mistake shadows for reality. In Diderot's version of that trope, a protofilmic screen—a canvas—is suspended in the back of the cave and gives rise to another of his imaginary conversations, this time between the philosophe and his friend Baron Grimm, the publisher of the *Correspondance Littéraire*, into which a thorough description of the painting that is ostensibly the subject of the review, along with the narrative of the story of Coresus and Callirhoe on which it is based, is slyly inserted.[7] As if immersed in the dreamlike space of a darkened theater, the reader of this extended riff on Fragonard's painting is led to imagine it almost somatically, by dint of the literary device of the Platonic allegory, repurposed as a piece of ekphrastic art criticism. This is all to say that the reader of Diderot's *Salon* is induced to hallucinate "the scene in Fragonard's picture" for him- or herself, as a response not to seeing the painting but to reading the words on the page and what they summon up in the so-called "mind's eye." Once more, then, Diderot returns to the device of literary imagining *in lieu of* what we would now call pictorial analysis, in this case by creating a protocinematic experience on the page.[8]

I have summarized some of Diderot's reviews of paintings that belong to other genres besides still life—to landscape, portraiture, and genre and history painting—in order to point to a *contrast* between those extended pieces of imaginative writing and the much shorter form and less inventive matter-of-factness of his discussions of Chardin's still-life paintings (though there are some important continuities as well). But before I get to those bits of still-life description, I want to make a point about Diderot's art criticism more broadly. Diderot has been described alternately as simply a bad art critic, as a champion of what Michael Fried calls the "absorptive" value in eighteenth-century French painting, and as a vivid describer of Chardin's work.[9] I disagree with all of these assessments. Instead, I would argue that Diderot's most elaborate pieces of criticism address the problem of ekphrastic writing head-on, with full and deliberate self-consciousness, but that that form of writing breaks down when confronted with the genre of still life as practiced by Chardin.

The Greek term *ekphrasis* dates back to the Hellenistic period, when it designated the kind of rhetorical exercises that young men of high-ranking families were set by their tutors, in which the orator would try to conjure up a scene, a place, a person, an event, or an object for a listening audience purely by means of vivid verbal evocations; only much later—in the twentieth century—did it come to mean poetry (or prose) that was specifically concerned with the description of art objects.[10] Hellenistic, Roman, and Byzantine writers concurred: "Ecphrasis is descriptive language," aimed at producing "a vivid impression of *all-but-seeing* what is described."[11] An ekphrasis "should almost create seeing through . . . hearing";[12] "what is elaborated in ecphrasis . . . brings before the eyes those things with which the words are concerned, and all but makes [us] spectators."[13] In sum, an ekphrasis should produce "a vivid impression of *all but seeing what is described*. . . . If the language is clear and vivid, what is said is changed from being heard to being seen; for *the language inscribes what is described in the eyes of the spectators and paints the truth in the imagination*."[14] This, we might say, is exactly what Diderot was trying to do in the eighteenth century, on the published page rather than as a public orator, in such a way that what came before the mind's eye was an experience of a scene, a place, a person, an event, or an object rather than of the painting that represented it—which is to say, he was attempting to create an image in and for the imagination (defined by the *Oxford English Dictionary* as "the power or capacity to form internal images . . . of objects and situations not actually present to the senses") by literary rather than pictorial means, rivaling and replacing the painting rather than rendering it per se.

\+ + + +

Among the most famous of early ekphrastic writing was the so-called *Imagines* by the third-century Philostratus the Elder, in which an entire gallery of pictures—possibly an imaginary one—was created for and in the "mind's eye" of the reader. Within that context, some of the most sensually vivid passages were devoted to still life.[15] This was remarkably *not* the case, however, in Diderot's *Salons*, when in the face of Chardin's still-life paintings, and in spite of his honest admiration for the painter and his work, most of Diderot's usual loquacity seemed to desert him. The most extensive of his pieces about Chardin occurred in the *Salon* of 1763, regarding the *Still Life with Jar of Olives* (figure 5) shown that year, in which Diderot began by asserting Chardin's status as a colorist:

> *This one is a painter; this one is a colorist.*
>
> At the Salon there are several little pictures by Chardin; almost all of them represent fruit together with the accessories of a meal. It is Nature itself; the objects come off of the canvas and are of such truthfulness that the eye is fooled.
>
> The one that you see when you go up the stairway merits the most attention. *On a table the artist has placed a vase of old Chinese porcelain, two biscuits, a jar filled with olives, a basket of fruit, two glasses half full of wine, a Seville orange and a paté.*
>
> To see the pictures of others, it seems as if I have to make myself a pair of eyes; in order to see those of Chardin, all I have to do is rely on the eyes that Nature gave me and that serve me well.
>
> If I wanted a child of mine to pursue painting, that is the picture I would buy. "Copy that for me, I would tell him, and copy it again." But perhaps Nature itself is not more difficult to copy.
>
> *It's that this porcelain vase is really made of porcelain; it's that these olives are really separated from the eye by the water in which they swim; it's that one has only to take those biscuits and eat them, open that orange and squeeze it, take that glass of wine and drink it, peel those fruits, put the knife to that paté.*
>
> This painter understands the harmony of colors and reflections. *O Chardin! It is not white, red, or black that you mix on your palette: it is the very substance of the objects, it is air and light that you put on the tip of your brush and attach to the canvas.*[16]

Faced with Chardin's still life, Diderot condenses the themes of his much longer and more elaborate pieces of ekphrasis into a short disquisition on Chardin's naturalism, contenting himself with a slightly vague inventory of the objects represented, and a riff on the relationship between the substances of which those objects are constructed and the pigments of which the painting is made: from the opening about painterly color, we proceed to the naming of things, to the optics of seeing them and the difficulty of copying Art versus Nature, thence into the substances of porcelain, water, pastry, fruit, wine, and paté, to conclude with a return to color, and the summarizing rhetorical move of proposing that the colors that are mixed on the palette are transformed by Chardin into "the very substance of the objects," as well as the "air and light" that surrounds them, which are attached to the canvas by the tip of Chardin's brush.

In the same review, Diderot proceeds as follows:

> *One understands nothing of this magic.* These are thick strata of color applied one on top of the other whose effect blooms up from the bottom to the top layer. In some cases one would say that it was *a vapor that had been exhaled onto the canvas;* in other instances that *a light foam had been thrown there.* [Artists] could explain this to you better than I, and even make you feel the effect on your eyes. *Approach and everything becomes blurry, flattens out and disappears; distance yourself, everything is created and properly reproduced.*
>
> *They tell me that Greuze, in going up to the Salon and coming upon [a] painting by Chardin . . . , looked at it and passed on, heaving a profound sigh. That praise is shorter and worth more than mine.*[17]

Thus, having developed the themes of copying, the optics, and the trompe l'oeil of naturalistic mimesis, the substance of color versus the substances of things, Diderot finishes by making several other observations to which I want to attend. He speaks to the distance of the viewer from the painting—and here he seems to call on a *viewer* more than a reader—as he or she moves close to and farther away from it: this would become a much-used trope of art criticism in the nineteenth century, particularly in the face of

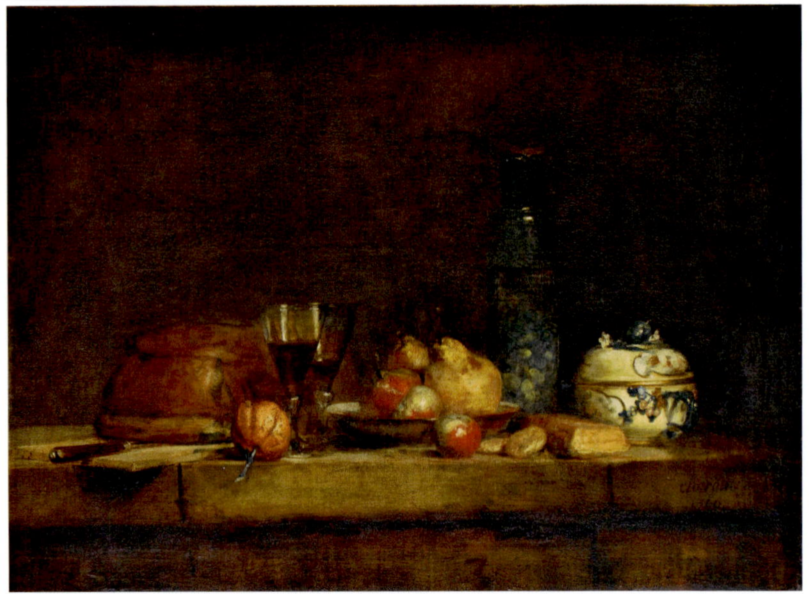

Figure 5. Jean-Baptiste-Siméon Chardin, *Still Life with Jar of Olives*, 1760. Oil on canvas. 28 × 38 1/2 in. (71 × 98 cm). Louvre. © RMN-Grand Palais / Art Resource, NY.

Impressionist painting. But more importantly, he also remarks on qualities of airiness, foaminess, and blurriness: vapor that has been exhaled, foam that has been cast onto the canvas surface, the blur that seems to result—all of which build on the idea of painting with air and light as much as with liquid and solid substance, an idea to which I will return later.

Most important of all, however, I want to signal Diderot's comments about not understanding the "magic" of Chardin's way of painting, and about heaving a sigh—as he claims that Greuze did—in front of it. Here the *philosophe* unwontedly celebrates the brevity, indeed the wordlessness of such a response—as if the appropriate reaction to such a painting was to be struck dumb by it. In fact, I would go so far as to say that here Diderot seems to champion two related but different kinds of failure: the failure to comprehend the painter's technique, and the failure to verbalize. He seems almost proud of the first failure—it marks him as a man of letters rather than of manual craft—in spite of how important technical explanations and illustrations were in the encyclopedic project that he oversaw. And about the second failure, he performs a sort of self-critical modesty—as if acknowledging, in advance, that all of the verbalizing about paintings that would become his art-critical trademark was both futile and excessive. It is the genre of still life that makes him admit that still life—*Chardin's* still life—confounds and silences him, as if the muteness of the objects in Chardin's still-life paintings had produced in Diderot a corresponding loss of words, an uncharacteristic inarticulacy. And as if still life—*Chardin's* still life—made him realize that he was addressing potential viewers, rather than readers: perhaps reading could *not*, after all, substitute for viewing. For a moment at least, the central fiction of ekphrasis, the literary production of an image in the imagination, came undone: still life—*Chardin's* still life—effectively brought ekphrasis to a standstill.

As for the painting itself, the *Still Life with Jar of Olives* that was the object of Diderot's impasse, it is more than double the size of the contemporaneous *Glass of Water and Coffeepot*—which, since it was not exhibited at the Salon, was never written about by Diderot—and much less simple in its arrangement. Instead it is marked by compositional complexity and a multiplicity of objects, from the knife under the paté at left to the tin-glazed casserole pot on the right: all of which Diderot had enumerated, though not entirely correctly, and not in any particular order. The painting represents a mix of old and new styles of earthenware glazing—which is to say of the more rustic and the more refined, the latter an imitation of porcelain, not the actual porcelain to which Diderot alludes in his review. It also includes two kinds of glass: the pair of stemmed goblets, probably made of then newly fashionable English flint glass, and the simpler olive jar, made of a dark blue-green glass that had been manufactured in France since the sixteenth century.[18]

In the Salon of 1765—the same Salon in which Diderot wrote so lengthily and fancifully about Greuze's *Girl with a Dead Bird* and Fragonard's *Coresus and Callirhoe*—Chardin had eight still-life paintings on view. After remarking, "Here you go again, great magician, with your *silent* arrangements . . . in which the air circulates around your objects" (and which nonetheless "speak eloquently"), Diderot took them one by one and devoted a brief paragraph—often just a sentence or two in length—to each of them.[19] The *Wild Duck with Olive Jar* (figure 6) and the *Basket of Plums* (figure 7) were among those eight still-life paintings. About the *Wild Duck*, which contains many of the same things found in the earlier *Still Life with Olive Jar*, Diderot began by remarking, "If it's true that no connoisseur can dispense with owning at least one Chardin, this is the one to go after." He goes on:

> Hang a duck by one leg. On a buffet underneath, imagine biscuits both whole and broken, a corked jar full of olives, a painted and covered china tureen, a lemon, a napkin that's been unfolded and carelessly flung down, a paté on a rounded wooden board, and glass half filled with wine . . . *The biscuits are yellow, the jar is green, the handkerchief is white, the wine red, and the juxtaposition of this yellow, this green, this white, this red* refreshes the eyes with a harmony that couldn't be bettered.[20]

About the much simpler *Basket of Plums*, Diderot merely wrote, "Place on a stone bench a wicker basket full of plums, for which a paltry string serves as a handle, and scatter around it some walnuts, two or three cherries, and some bunches of grapes."[21]

The two paintings in question represent the two ends of the Chardinian spectrum, running from complexity to the utmost simplicity. They also are

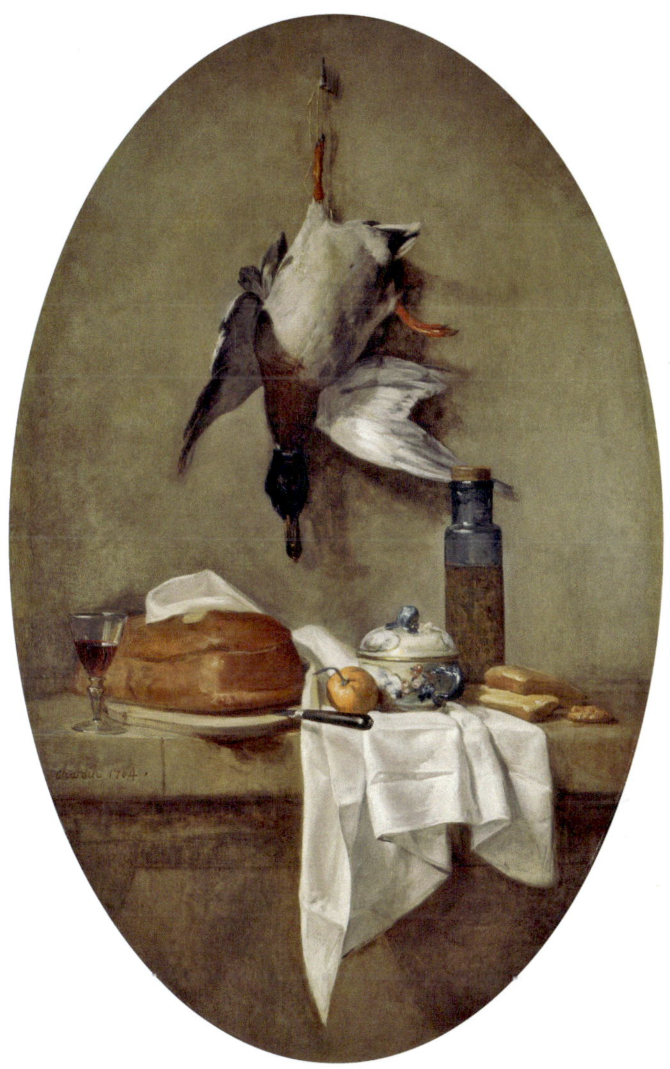

Figure 6. Jean-Baptiste-Siméon Chardin, *Wild Duck with Olive Jar*, 1764. Oil on canvas. 60 × 37¾ in. (153 × 96 cm). Courtesy of Michele and Donald D'Amour Museum of Fine Arts, Springfield, Massachusetts, The James Philip Gray Collection. Photography by David Stansbury.

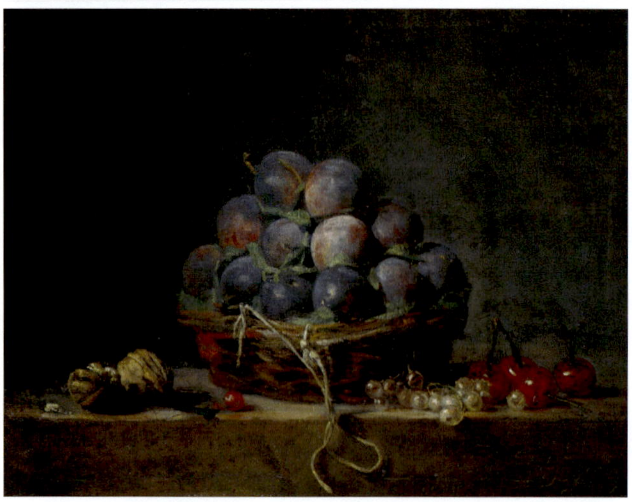

Figure 7. Jean-Baptiste-Siméon Chardin, *Basket of Plums*, 1765. Oil on canvas. 12 ¾ × 16 ½ in. (32.4 × 41.9 cm). Chrysler Museum of Art, Norfolk. Gift of Walter P. Chrysler, Jr.

markedly different in scale: the *Wild Duck* is even bigger than the *Still Life with Jar of Olives*, while the dimensions of the *Basket of Plums* are roughly the same as those of the *Glass of Water and Coffee Pot*. But both paintings are treated similarly by Diderot, who, after acknowledging that the *Wild Duck* was a commodity for sale—an object to be owned—goes on to issue injunctions to the viewer to make still-life arrangements of his or her own, consisting of the same objects represented in each of the two paintings. And in both cases, he finishes by a return to the question of the colors of Chardin's palette; in the case of the *Basket of Plums*, the short inventory of the objects portrayed in it that I have quoted above leads into a longer, more general discussion of the painter's colorism and painterly handling, along with questions of genre and style.

For Diderot's discussion of *Basket of Plums*, which terminates his treatment of Chardin's series of paintings in the Salon of 1765, ends by addressing the inimitability of Chardin's way of painting, asking the question: "Can you think of a literary style suited to anything and everything?" "The genre of Chardin's painting," he concludes, "is the least demanding one, but no living painter, not even Vernet, is as perfectly accomplished in the one he's chosen."[22] Thus Diderot acknowledges a distinction between literary and pictorial style, once more throwing up his hands at the inutility of saying more: Chardin's still lifes may be eloquent, as he proclaimed somewhat contradictorily, but they are also "silent." As such, they effectively silence Diderot, the *philosophe* who wanted to explain everything but had to resort to the notion of "magic" to account for Chardin's paintings, in front of which he stands agape.

\+ + + +

Basket of Plums was a reiteration of an earlier painting representing its plums paired with a glass of water similar to the one in the 1760 still life that is the centerpiece of this discussion (figure 8); that earlier painting seems to have appeared in the Salon of 1759, the earliest of the Salons about which Diderot had written, but without mentioning any individual paintings by Chardin: all he had said then was "For still lifes, the great master is Chardin, as always."[23] If we take a quick tour back through Chardin's still lifes, to explore his object choices and his variations on their combination and placement, we will find that the earliest instance of a basket of plums occurs in a still life from 1728 (figure 9), presently in the Frick Collection, in which there also appears a plain glass of water, a bottle made of the coal-fused black glass invented in England in the seventeenth century, and what I suppose are two loaves of crusty bread, all on a tilting, rustic ledge. As it happens, this latter painting is the subject of a beautiful ekphrasis by the ceramic artist Edmund

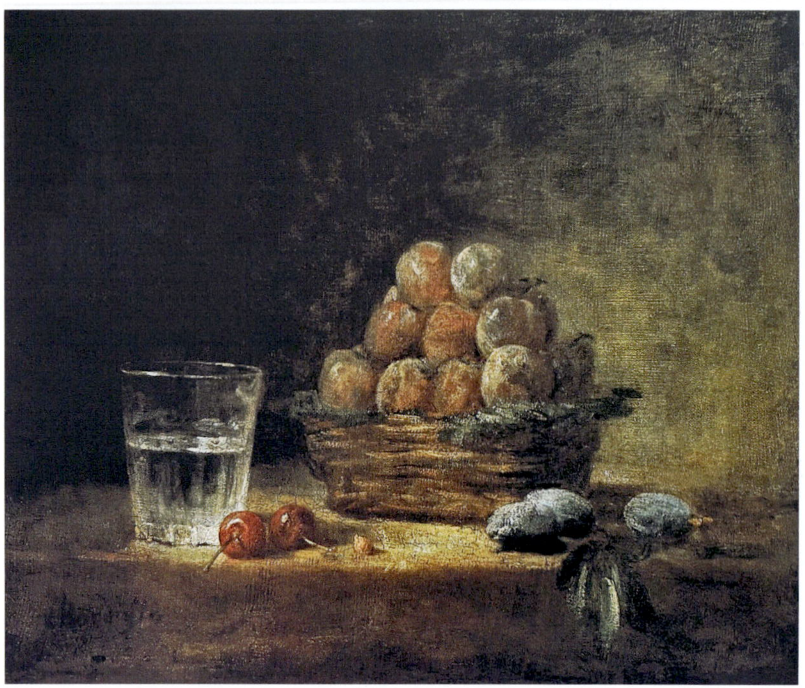

Figure 8. Jean-Baptiste-Siméon Chardin, *Basket of Plums*, 1759. Oil on canvas. 12 3/4 × 16 1/2 in. (32.4 × 41.9 cm). Musée des beaux arts, Rennes.

de Waal—part of a recent compendium of ekphrastic pieces by different artists and writers on works of art in the Frick Collection—in which he writes that "Chardin paints this act of moving things around," before enumerating those still-life paintings in which plums are found: "Chardin paints *A Bowl of Plums*. He then paints *Still Life with Plums*. Then *Basket of Plums and Glass of Water*. Then *Basket of Plums*." Before concluding with a quote from a poem about eating plums by William Carlos Williams, de Waal remarks, "We have to pay attention. Some of the plums are purple, some are green Mirabelles. *The glass of water looks the same*, I think, in most of his pictures, but the bloom

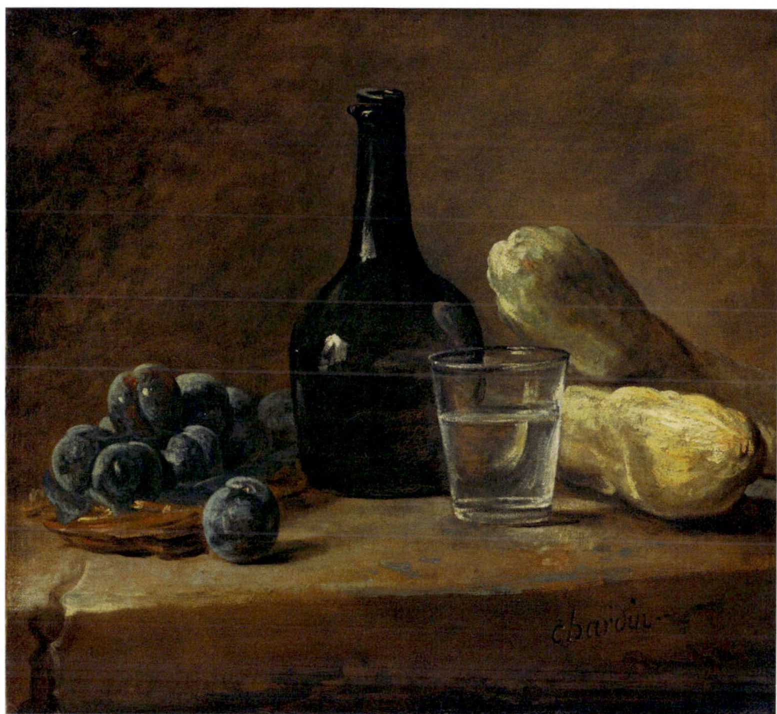

Figure 9. Jean-Baptiste-Siméon Chardin, *Still Life with Plums*, ca. 1730. Oil on canvas. 17 3/4 × 19 3/4 in. (45.1 × 50.2 cm). The Frick Collection, New York. Image © The Frick Collection.

on each plum is evanescent and immortal."[24] Which is to say that, among the objects to which Chardin returned over and over again, the glass of water had a recurring permanence that the plums—and other mounded fruit such as peaches and strawberries—did not; it was even more endlessly repeatable than they were.

A 1933 inventory counted "at least 140 paintings featuring objects made of glass, including about a hundred bottles, eighty drinking glasses and about fifty assorted decanters, jars and bottles" in Chardin's oeuvre.[25] Among those eighty drinking glasses—mostly from the late part of Chardin's still-life

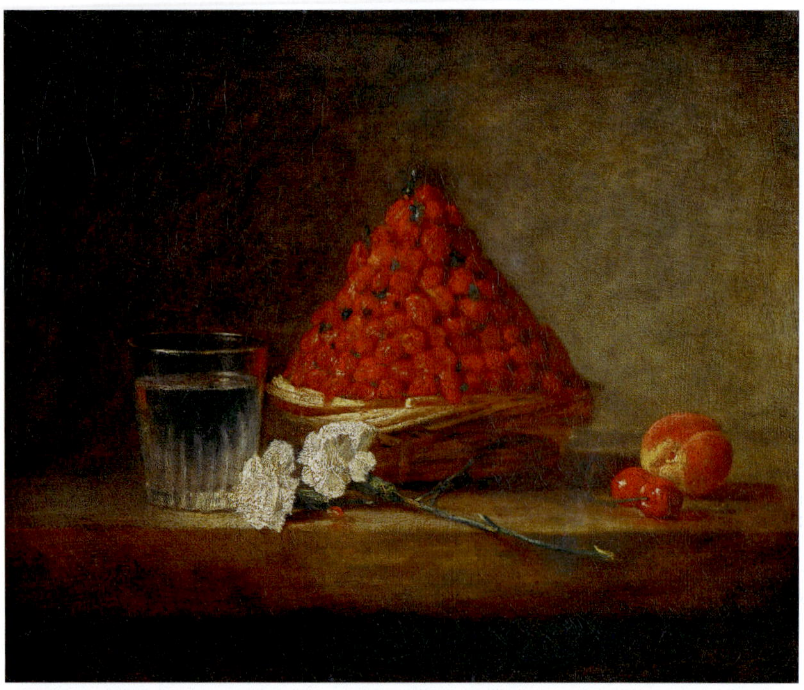

Figure 10. Jean-Baptiste-Siméon Chardin, *Basket of Wild Strawberries*, 1761. Oil on canvas. 15 × 18 1/8 in. (38 × 46 cm). Louvre. Erich Lessing / Art Resource, NY.

practice—we find those in the 1759 *Basket of Plums* just mentioned, the 1760 *Glass of Water and Coffeepot* with which I begin and end, the rightly famous *Basket of Wild Strawberries*, which was shown in the Salon of 1761 without receiving any commentary from Diderot (figure 10), and a pair of still lifes, now in the Louvre, from 1768: the *Basket of Peaches* and the *Pears, Walnuts and Glass of Wine* (figures 11, 12), which both contain the projecting knife, mentioned at the outset, that was so ubiquitous in the history of still-life painting. The drinking glasses in those last two paintings contain wine rather than water, and one of them appears to be made of the same blue-green glass

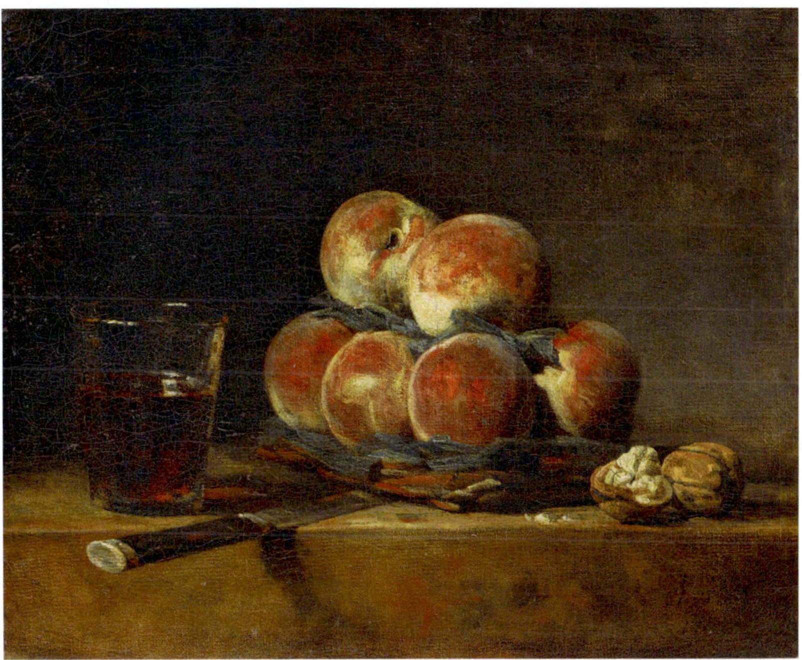

Figure 11. Jean-Baptiste-Siméon Chardin, *Basket of Peaches*, 1768. Oil on canvas. 12 5/8 × 15 3/8 in. (32 × 39 cm). Louvre. © RMN-Grand Palais / Art Resource, NY.

as that of the olive jar in the painting discussed by Diderot in the *Salon* of 1763, but in both cases the drinking glasses have the same simple shape as they have in the early *Still Life with Plums* in the Frick Collection, the Rennes *Basket of Plums*, the *Glass of Water and Coffee Pot*, and the *Basket of Wild Strawberries*. (It is worth remarking, here, that for its part, the *Glass of Water and Coffee Pot* began its life with a similar basket of strawberries featured in its composition in lieu of the coffee pot painted over it, as X-rays of the painting now reveal.)[26]

One other late still life that includes a drinking glass is worth adducing—this one featuring a stemmed glass turned upside down in a wine cooler, so

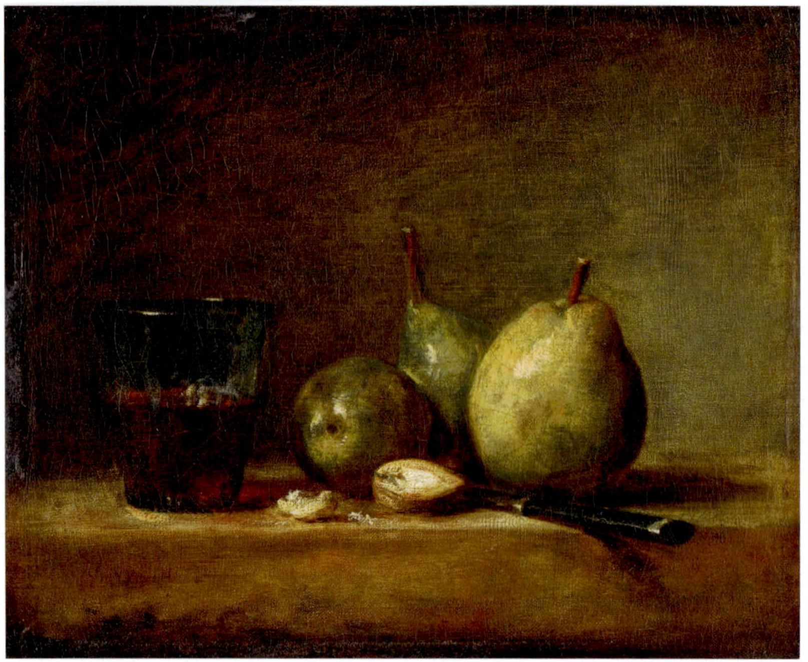

Figure 12. Jean-Baptiste-Siméon Chardin, *Pears, Walnuts, and Glass of Wine*, 1768. Oil on canvas. 13 × 16 1/8 in. (33 × 41 cm). Louvre. © 2010 GrandPalaisRmn (musée du Louvre) / Stéphane Maréchalle.

that one can see its stem and base—the *Basket of Peaches with Grapes and Wine Cooler* of 1759 (figure 13): I shall have occasion to return to this outlier in Chardin's preoccupation with drinking glasses filled with water or wine, but always suggesting an interest in the relation between liquidity and the solidity of glass, not to mention, in the case of the water-filled glasses, between the colorless clarity of the one and the equally colorless transparency of the other. For now, let me point to one other privileged item, the repeated silver goblet that we find among Chardin's array of object preoccu-

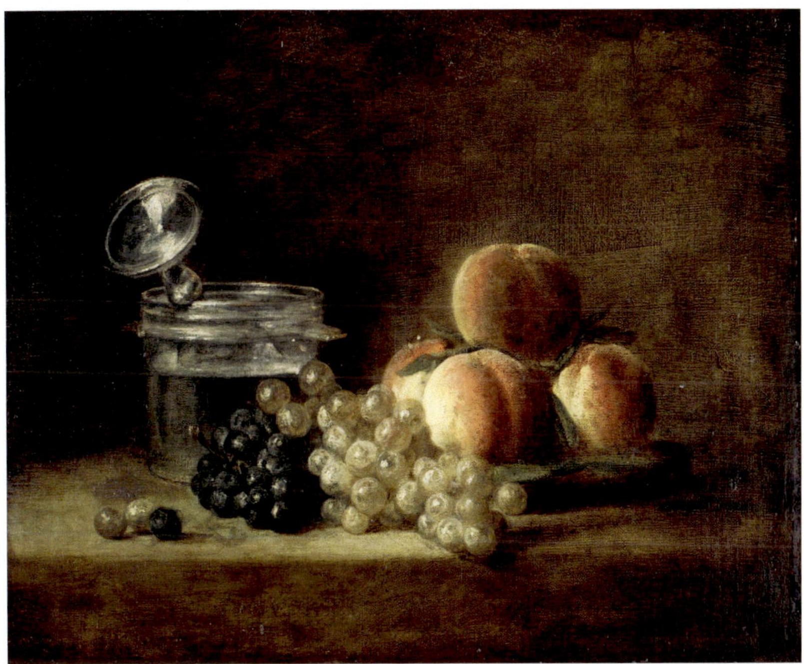

Figure 13. Jean-Baptiste-Siméon Chardin, *Basket of Peaches with Grapes and Wine Cooler*, 1759. Oil on canvas. 15 × 18 1/8 in. (38 × 46 cm). Musée des beaux-arts, Rennes. © Rennes, Museum of Fine Arts—Jean-Manuel Salingue.

pations, which included black glass bottles, rustic bottles, and stoppered jars of various lighter hues of glass, flint-glass stemmed goblets, a gilt-edged liqueur decanter, a repeated, sprig-patterned water pitcher with a hinged lid, a white tin-glazed earthenware teapot and another dark-glazed one, a little Delft bud vase, a Meissen tureen and a silver tureen, and a pewter jug, usually together with various arrangements of fruits and nuts. I single out the silver goblet, as it appears in a variety of still lifes from 1728 to 1768—such as the Getty *Still Life with Peaches, Silver Goblet, Grapes and Walnuts* of 1759–60,

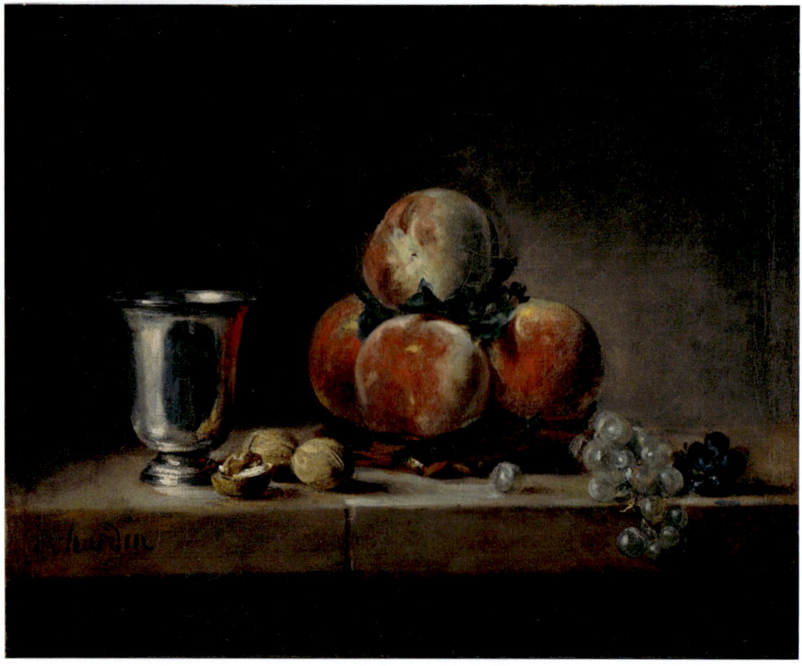

Figure 14. Jean-Baptiste-Siméon Chardin, *Still Life with Peaches, Silver Goblet, Grapes and Walnuts*, 1759–60. Oil on canvas. 15 × 18 3/8 in. (38.1 × 46.7 cm). Getty.

or the 1768 *Silver Goblet* in the Louvre, where it appears next to a little bowl with an equally silver spoon in it (figures 14, 15)—because of the way Chardin insisted on showing off the silver sheen and reflective capacities of its surface. In *The Silver Goblet*, that silver surface not only reflects the apples situated between the goblet and the bowl, but also features along its rim gleams of the colors that make them up, as if to self-reflexively condense the Diderotian movement back and forth between the substances of things and the colors of the pigments used to render them. This happens very occasionally with the water glasses: in the *Basket of Wild Strawberries*, for instance, we see two touches of the red that makes up the mound of strawberries, one on

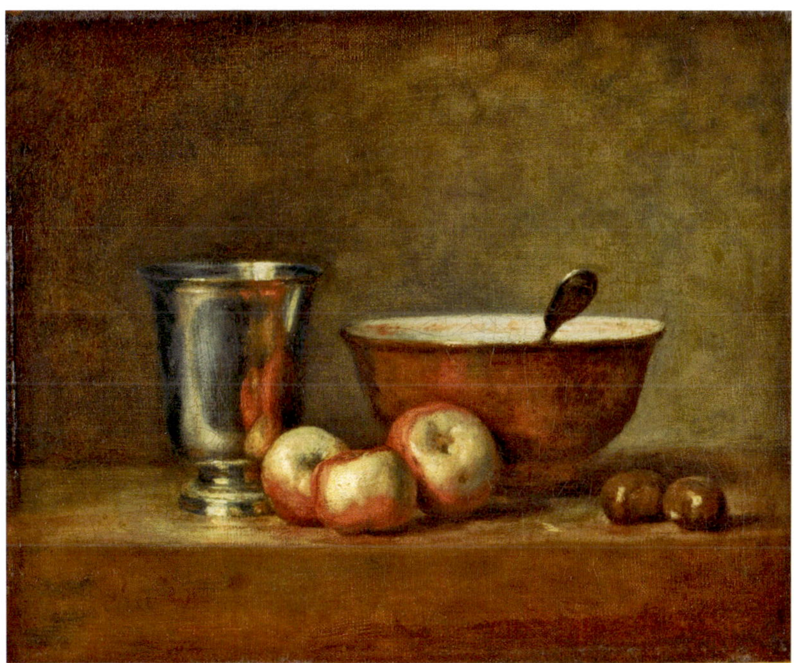

Figure 15. Jean-Baptiste-Siméon Chardin, *The Silver Goblet*, 1768. Oil on canvas. 13 × 16 1/4 in. (33 × 41 cm). Louvre.

either side of the water glass that sits to the left of it. More usually, however, it is the transparency of the glass that matters most, as it does in the *Glass of Water and Coffee Pot*, to which I now return.

\+ + + +

Diderot, too, was interested in glass and glassmaking; indeed, when he wrote his essay on "Art" for the *Encyclopedia*, and used that essay to argue for giving at least as much respect to what he termed the "mechanical" as to the so-called "liberal" arts, he cited glassmaking as one of two first prime examples (the other being papermaking).[27] In a moment, I shall return to

Chardin's glass, and to the long disquisition on glassmaking in Diderot's *Encyclopedia*. But for now, let me start with the greenish-brown-glazed earthenware coffeepot, and Diderot's own six-page account of the art of *fayence* (earthenware) in the *Encyclopedia*, illustrated with twelve plates published separately from the text to which they are matched, as was the case with all of the *Encyclopedia*'s illustrations.

Those plates commence with four representing works produced through the art of *fayence*, beginning with the very simplest, among the first of which we find the very coffeepot that is paired with the glass in Chardin's little painting. (Later sequences of plates are devoted, more generically, to the making of clay pottery, including a plate illustrating the production of a similar simple pot by the building up of coils. That sequence, by the way, is followed by one illustrating pewter pot making, and elsewhere we find a short section focused on the production of porcelain: the very crafts and materials that are exemplified by Chardin's object choices. Silver, as in the silver goblet that we have just seen in a number of Chardin's still lifes, also has a substantial entry, authored by Diderot, though most of it is dedicated to the mining and chemical aspect of the metal.) As for the essay by Diderot on the art of *fayence* that matches these plates, it is dedicated to the total explanation and demystification of the craft in all of its aspects, which was typical of what the *Encyclopedia* set out to accomplish across the board, and couldn't be more contrary to Diderot's expressions of technical befuddlement in the face of the "magic" of Chardin's painterly craft.

Beginning with the Italian origins of *fayence*, Diderot then describes the material makeup of the clay used in it, the digging up and sifting of that clay, the manner of throwing pots on the wheel (intensively manual in Diderot's repeated indications of the placement of hands, thumbs, and fingers), the preparing of the kiln, the firing and cooling of the pots, and then the glazing of them, finishing with a long series of recipes for different colors of glaze (including the mottled greenish brown seen on Chardin's coffeepot). Along the way, tools are named and explained, technical terminology is defined, and the figures in the plates are constantly referenced: as Diderot remarked, "it is easier to understand [a simple construction] by means of a glance at the figure than by a [verbal] description."[28] Which is to say, since the plates are in separate volumes from those containing the text of the *Encyclopedia*, that the reader has the options of reading the text without the illustrations, or of looking at the illustrations without reading the text, or, alternatively, of going to the trouble of working back and forth between them. But it is also to say that the visual—in the form of "the figure," at least—is given priority over the verbal in conducing the reader to "understand" how things are made.

In the first four plates (figures 16, 17), one sees the ascending order of complexity of the items produced by the art of *fayence:* it is notable both that Diderot stressed the simplest as those that are easiest to understand by way of visual illustration rather than verbal explanation, and that the simplest items were also those chosen by Chardin. I shall come back to that double point about simplicity momentarily. The remaining eight plates embody the structure of all of the illustrations in the *Encyclopedia*, sometimes more briefly and sometimes more extensively, even obsessively "encyclopedic" in their figuring not only of the products but also of the tools, the mechanics, the workers and workspaces, and the phases of production of any given work of artisanal "art," such as the glazed earthenware coffeepot, set next to the glass of water, in the *Glass of Water and Coffee Pot*.

As well as the emphasis on the manual nature of the craft of pot making, among the other important themes that are stressed in Diderot's article on *fayence* are the different states of matter involved in the production of earthenware, from the granularity of dirt and sand to the fluidity of slip and glaze to the hardening of earthen clay: in other words, the phase changes between liquid and solid and back again, along with the evaporation of water involved in the drying of earthenware. Additionally, the vitreous nature of glaze is

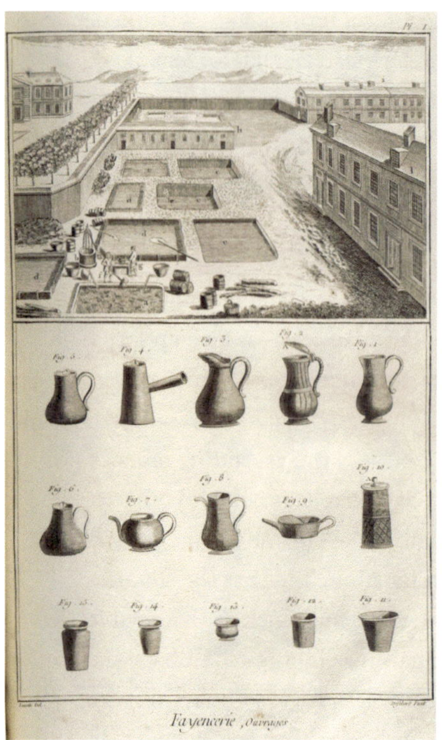

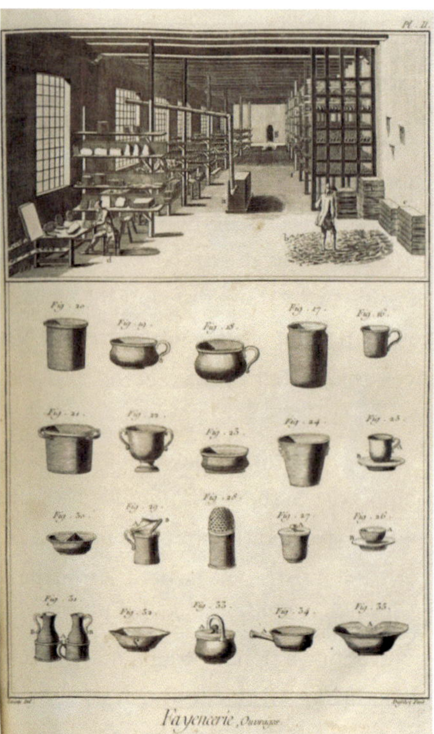

Figure 16. Diderot and d'Alembert, *Encyclopédie*, illustrations, 1762–77. *Fayencerie* (760–63). ARTFL Project, University of Chicago.

brought to the fore, glaze being the finishing touch that sits halfway between clay and glass, linking one to the other, and bringing out—bringing to the surface, quite literally—the glass-like quality of fired clay, or rather, the shared glassiness of glass, glaze, and clay (and even the bricks that make up the ovens in which vessels are heated, which is stressed in the longer article on glassmaking, to which I will turn in a moment, and which is referenced repeatedly in that last portion of Diderot's article on *fayence* that is dedicated to glazing).[29] And finally, Diderot also accents the painterly nature of the

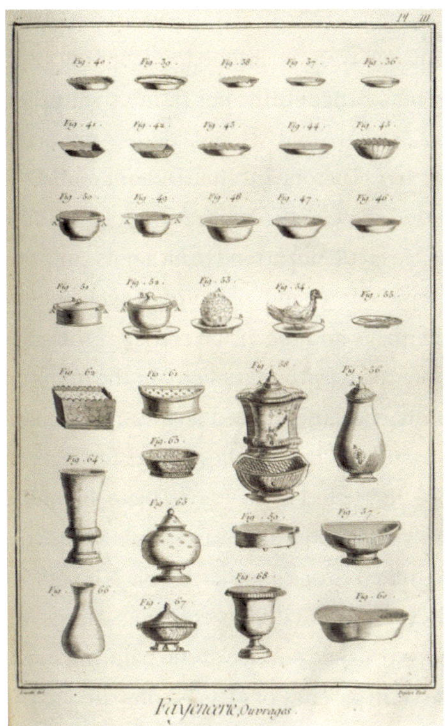

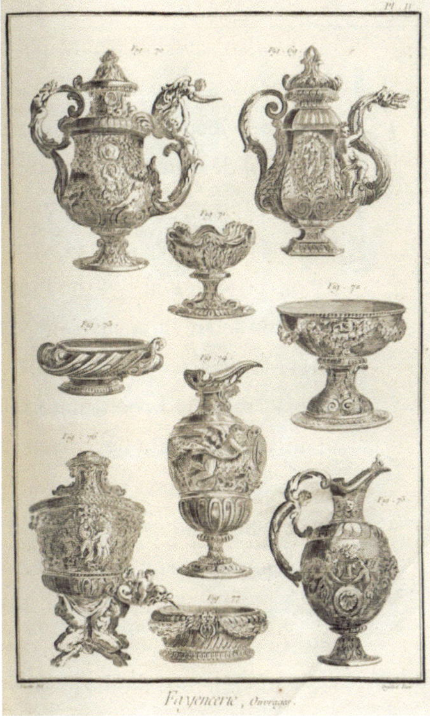

Figure 17. Diderot and d'Alembert, *Encyclopédie*, illustrations, 1762–77. *Fayencerie* (760–63). ARTFL Project, University of Chicago.

mixing and applying of colored glazes, thereby linking the craft of *fayence* to the art of painting.

Yet despite that, Diderot could not find a way to talk about paintings by Chardin in which *fayence* appeared, in front of which both his ekphrastic aptitude in writing about painting and his explanatory zeal with regard to the *techne* of crafted objects failed him, as if Chardin's paintings fell into the gap between the two. Why was that so? Perhaps because of the distinction that Diderot himself had made, in his entry on "Art" in the *Encyclopedia*, between the so-called "liberal" and "mechanical" arts, between which we might also say that Chardin's paintings were positioned, occupying both categories at once—or perhaps neither of them fully, but rather the liminal space between them—thus putting pressure on both of Diderot's preferred modes of dealing with Art and the arts. That meant that Diderot could *not* find the terms with which to attend to some of the key features of a still life like the *Glass of Water and Coffee Pot*. He could not attend to either its simplicity or the simplicity of the items depicted, in spite of having advocated for both the self-evidence of the visual image and the visual clarity of the simplest of items. He could not articulate the way the simplicity of the items on display rendered their material properties and crafted shapes much more vividly than would have been the case had Chardin chosen ornate pieces of glass- or earthenware, such as those illustrated in the fourth plate matching his article on *fayence*. He could not speak about the way simple items like these, simultaneously opposed and linked to one another, display the differences *and* the similarities of their respectively vitreous colored surfaces, all within the single, but multicolored, varnished surface of the painting itself. He could not talk about the way the transparency of glass is compared to the opacity of earthenware in such a work, nor about the way a painting like *Glass of Water and Coffee Pot* puts in play the related and differentiated properties of liquid and solid, water, glass, and clay, or the related painterlinesses of mottled, marbled glaze and oil painting: all precisely the kinds of things he attended to in his article on *fayence*. Or to put it more briefly, where a "figure" of a "simple [earthenware] construction" was apparently transparent, "by means of a glance," to his (and the reader's) "understanding," an oil painting of the same "simple construction" simply was not.

\+ + + +

I come now to the glass in that same painting, and the other similar glasses in other still lifes by Chardin, which is where I want to end. In a brief entry on "drinking glasses" by the Chevalier Louis de Jaucourt—who was the most prolific contributor to the *Encyclopedia*, writing about eighteen thousand of its articles—a simple description of a "verre à boire" is given: "a vessel made of simple glass or crystal, ordinarily in the form of an inverted cone, which one uses for drinking all manner of liquors. The glass has three parts, the chalice, the button [or the base] and the stem, which are separately worked. Nothing is more industrious than the art of blowing those parts, of making openings in two out of three of them and joining them to the third; but this work can only be understood by seeing it."[30] This description of a drinking glass evidently refers to stemware, such as those in the painting of the *Jar of Olives*, or the one that is turned upside down in the painting of the *Wine Cooler*—as if to show us the separate parts of a stemmed glass—rather than the simpler glasses so often preferred by Chardin. But, because of both their own simplicity as shapes and the greater simplicity of the compositions in which they find themselves—so that they are not lost in a jumble of multiple objects—those simpler glasses allow us to better "under[stand] by seeing" what we are looking at and to focus on their glassiness as well as their containment of liquid, and so in those senses they also correspond better to Jaucourt's simple, straightforward, we might even say "transparent," description.

The simplicity of most of Chardin's glasses also returns us to the beginnings of a long tradition of the representation of glass in Western still-life painting, going all the way back to the first-century Roman frescoes at Oplontis and Herculaneum, and culminating in all the many elaborate representations of glassware in Dutch seventeenth-century painting, such as the still lifes by Willem Claesz. Heda (of which the 1634 *Still Life with Roemer* in Rotterdam [see figure 21] is just one), where highly worked German glass keeps company with just as highly worked silver and shows off its properties of reflection and refraction, transparency and high polish, and fragility and breakability, as well as its capacity to hold liquid, but so complexly entwined with its own decorative detailing and the artificed materialities of the other items with which it keeps such multifarious company, that those properties get somewhat lost in the mix. What Chardin's simple glasses do is to isolate out the transparency of glass, along with the capacity of its hollow solid to hold liquid, which had also been the focus of ancient emphasis too: as if, from the very beginning, the key attraction of glass was its transparency, along with its movement between the states of solid and liquid. And as if, from the beginning, the attraction of *painting* glass had resided in those two qualities as well: the basic illusion of transparency, on the one hand, which by the Renaissance was tied to the notion of the picture plane as a notionally transparent window through which one looks, and on the other hand, the combination of fluid binder and pulverized mineral that paint pigment was (and sometimes still is), and which hardens from its liquid to its solid state when it dries.[31]

The *Encyclopedia* contains multiple entries on glass and glassmaking: three pages on the history of glass in general by Jaucourt; four anonymously authored pages on the glass used in the making of spectacles; a page by d'Alembert on what we would now call scientific glass (i.e., glass used for making optical devices such as prisms, microscopes, and telescopes); a short paragraph on faceted glass; two pages by Jaucourt on glass used in lens making; another two pages, also by Jaucourt, on "turned" glass; several pages dedicated to drawing or etching on glass; and so on. But the anonymously authored essay dedicated to *verrerie*, the glass-making industry in all its aspects—likely by a team of authors which may have included Diderot himself—is some fifty-four pages long, including a long section on the making of bottle glass, and an even longer section on the making of flat glass for windows and mirrors—which had become a national specialty and was celebrated as such in the *Encyclopedia*. There are fifty-four plates in all dedicated to *verrerie*. (Compare that to the *Encyclopedia*'s eight plates dedicated to the fine art of *peinture* [painting].) As in the *fayence* entry, so in the *verrerie* essay with its matching plates every aspect of different kinds of glassmaking is covered, just much more extensively: ovens and workshops are shown and explicated, phases of labor are extensively explained and illustrated, and tools, gear, and even workshop garments are referenced and represented. Indeed, as elsewhere in the *Encyclopedia*, the combination of verbal explication (in one volume) and visual illustration (kept separate in another volume) often redounds into redundancy, well exceeding what was strictly necessary for the elucidation of the craft, and indexing the illustrational mania that the explanatory zeal of this quintessential Enlightenment project had generated.[32] Nowhere is that excess more evident than in the multiple entries on glass and glassmaking, and the many illustrations to which they refer.

In particular, the steps in the turning, shaping, and blowing of glass are comprehensively—and indeed, repetitively—depicted (figures 18, 19). And then they are recapitulated, for the long essay on *verrerie* ends with a short section on "common glass" and another one on crystal made with potash, in which all the steps in blowing and finishing glass are summarized once more for good measure:

> One begins by taking or picking up some [molten] crystal with the cane, which is a little hot, and whose end the assistant puts in the [molten] material. He turns the cane, the glass attaches itself; if he hasn't taken enough the first time, he reiterates the same operation: as soon as it is properly done, he rolls the glass and blows into it; if the piece is shaped, fluted, and/or with a stem, be blows it in a copper mold; then he marks the neck with an iron: if it is a carafe, he gives it to another worker who reheats it in the workroom; then putting in a wooden mold, he blows it to the size it should have; he sticks the end on with pincers; . . . he separates the carafe from the cane; he attaches it to the end of the rod; he reheats the end in the workroom; then he sits on the bench and with the iron he fashions the neck, while turning it and applying the iron inside and out; continuously turning the rod.[33]

I will return to the part of this narration of the phases of glassmaking that concerns the blowing of air into the molten material, and close with it. But

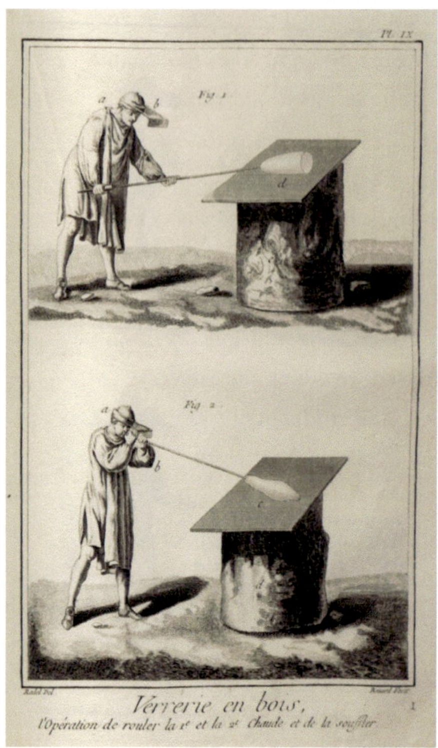

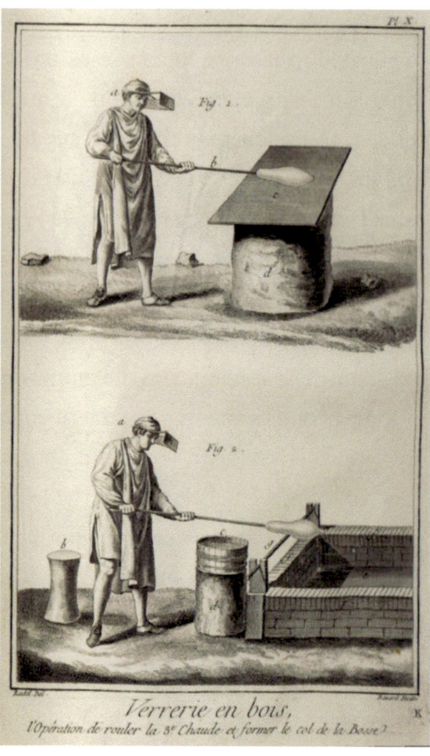

Figure 18. Diderot and d'Alembert, *Encyclopédie*, *Verrerie en bois*, plates IX, X (7602–3). ARTFL Project, University of Chicago.

first, let me bear down once more on the vexed intersection between the *Encyclopedia*, Diderot's art criticism, and Chardin's still-life practice.

In Jaucourt's entry on the history of glass, the transparency of the material is emphasized above all else, along with the phase changes of matter that it embodies.[34] At the beginning of that entry, Jaucourt describes the material of glass this way: "hard, fragile, transparent, smooth and incorruptible matter that no substance can alter. Only fire, to which it owes its birth, has power over it; it at least has the capacity to make it change its form, as it can

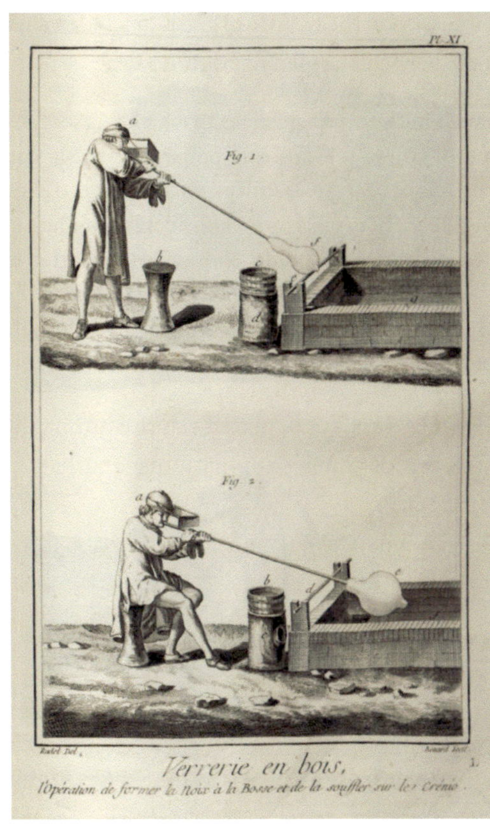

Figure 19. Diderot and d'Alembert, *Encyclopédie*, *Verrerie en bois*, plate XI (2604). ARTFL Project, University of Chicago.

prepare it in the first place by the fusion of sand, vitreous stones and alkaline salt." Speaking of the phenomenon of a "fiery stream [of molten glass, which begins as a] brilliant, foaming flow that in cooling takes on a solid, diaphanous form," which was first observed by chance some "1000 years before the birth of Christ," Jaucourt proceeds to meditate on this "beautiful and transparent" material and the ancient efforts, from Aristotle to Lucretius, to explain its transparency, before going on to summarize alchemical efforts to perfect and simulate it, and its importance to the modern sciences of chemistry and physics. His short essay on the history of glass concludes with the following brief remark about the vitreous glazing of chinaware:

> *Glass* as we have just described it in the different states to which it is susceptible, in disguising itself in the form of brilliant and polished varnish, can also furnish the arts with a means of coating beautiful objects that the taste for luxury has for more than a century turned into a considerable branch of commerce; by that I mean Chinese porcelain, which Europeans have tried to imitate by astonishing new feats of manufacturing, not by the nature of the porcelain paste itself, but by the nobility of its contours, the beauty of its design, the vivacity of its colors, and the brilliance of its finish.[35]

Thus, once more, the materials of glass and fired, glazed clay are intimately tied together, as they are, by means of comparison with one another, in Chardin's *Glass of Water and Coffee Pot.*

In his book *The System of Objects* (1968), Jean Baudrillard wrote about the "Model Material: Glass" as follows:

> Glass is . . . both the material used and the ideal to be achieved, both end and means . . . *the miracle of a rigid fluid—a content that is also a container, and hence the basis of a transparency between the two* . . . with its indestructibility, immunity to decay, colourlessness, odourlessness, and so on, glass exists at a sort of zero level of matter: glass is to matter as a vacuum is to air. . . . Glass is the basis of a transparency without transition: *we see, but cannot touch. . . . at once magical and frustrating . . . Glass works exactly like atmosphere . . . It interposes itself in its transparency,* just as the system of atmosphere does in its abstract consistency, between the materiality of things and the materiality of needs.[36]

"The miracle of a rigid fluid—a content that is also a container, and hence the basis of a transparency between the two": here Baudrillard speaks to the "magical" qualities of glass, an "amorphous solid" that remains a liquid at the molecular level, and so, when it holds liquid, as it does in the case of Chardin's *Glass of Water and Coffee Pot,* it is exactly "a content that is also a container," and/or vice versa.[37] And thus Chardin's decision to fill his glass with water rather than wine might be seen as a way of equating the liquid with the solid that the material of glass holds in suspension. Equally, it might be understood as a way of doubling down on transparency, and of insisting on the equivalence between liquid and solid transparencies. And then, that "magical" glass also "works exactly like atmosphere," in that "it interposes itself in its transparency" such that "we see, but cannot touch": this is true, too, of Chardin's glass of water, which effectively crystallizes the invisible atmosphere that is everywhere in and around it. Which is also to say that its "frustrating" magic lies not only in its making visible of the invisible, and in its simultaneous constitution out of, and dissipation back into thin air, but also in its illusionism.

Baudrillard's attention to glass's transparency is at once literal and metaphorical. And his description of its transparency as a "secondary state of consciousness" as much as "the zero level on the scale of materials," so that it embodies a mental mode of abstraction and transcendence as much as a state of physical matter, certainly applies to the "transparency"—the simplicity, clarity, and self-evidence—of the *Encyclopedia*'s superabundance of descriptions, explanations, and illustrations, in which nothing, including the paper of the pages on which its plates were printed, is allowed to remain opaque to either the eye or the understanding. At the same metaphorical level, however, it also represents an area of simultaneous overlap and contradiction between Baudrillard's critique of the capitalist abstraction of "the system of atmosphere" and the aporia in Diderot's own rationality: for both circle ambiguously in and around the terrain of the "magical."[38] In contrast, the metaphorical notion of transparency describes Chardin's painting—along with the still-life tradition to which it belongs, and its long history of fascinated attention to the literal transparency of glass—rather less well. For evidently, the illusionism of Chardin's still lifes was thoroughly opaque to a philosophe like Diderot, who threw up his hands and spoke of magic while arguing for dumbfounded silence and a mystified sigh as the best reaction to it. Perhaps such a painting was eloquent, but its eloquence was something that Diderot could not translate into words, and so its objects remain resolutely mute. Though the "arts" represented in it could be explained, its "Art" could not, nor could it be rendered mentally visible or tangible by any ekphrastic flight of imagination that strayed away from its physical presence in front of an actual viewer's actual eyes.

\+ + + +

I conclude with a postscript that brings us back to the other state of matter involved in the production of glass: to air and airiness, and the use of breath to blow either glass or a soap bubble, the latter an act represented by Chardin three times over in and around 1734 (as in the Metropolitan's *Soap Bubbles*, figure 20), which is to say, well before either the *Encyclopedia* or Diderot's *Salons*.[39] Air—the most ubiquitous form of the gaseous state of matter, but also that which animates and ensouls animal life, in contrast to inert objects and substances—is what must circulate through the glassblowing atelier, as the "Verrerie" article in the *Encyclopedia* indicates repeatedly.[40] But of course, air is also what is blown into molten glass to shape it, as the *Encyclopedia*'s plates demonstrate. And air is what is blown through a straw into soapy water to form evanescent bubbles, as Chardin's painting shows, effectively comparing that act and the fragile transparency that it produces to the already blown glass, on the left side of the composition, that holds the soap in its foamy, liquid state, transformed from water's transparency into the milky opacity of soap suspended in water.

Recall Diderot's words about the *Jar of Olives:* speaking of "a vapor that had been exhaled" and of "a light foam that had been thrown there," he declared to Chardin that, in addition to "the very substance of the objects, it is air and light that you put on the tip of your brush and attach to the canvas." Thus air, too, is what Diderot describes as circulating through Chardin's still-life compositions, depositing a foam, as if blown by breath, onto

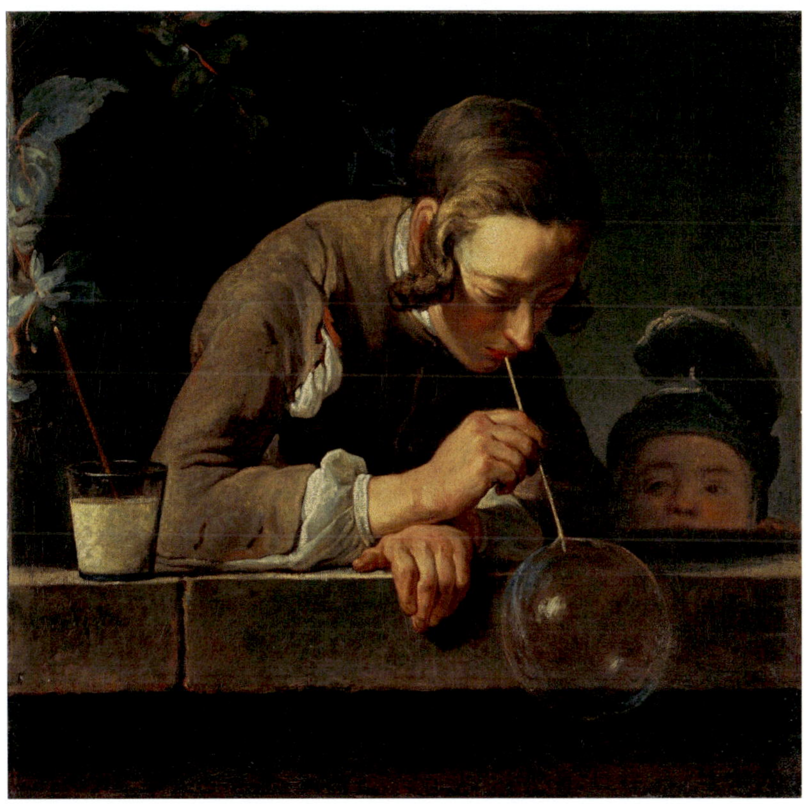

Figure 20. Jean-Baptiste-Siméon Chardin, *Soap Bubbles*, ca. 1733–34. Oil on canvas. 24 × 24 7/8 in. (61 × 63.2 cm). Metropolitan Museum of Art, Wentworth Fund, 1949, 49.24.

their surfaces: air, a form of sublimation, that seems to dematerialize the painting's matter and render it invisible or, at least, to allow the invisible to spread throughout and thoroughly interpenetrate the painting's visual field. Diderot's art-critical airiness speaks both to the transubstantiation that he seems to feel is the *effect* of the painting's illusionism and to his own frustrated desire to sublimate its materiality. Chardin's painterly airiness, by contrast, is tied to an act of material production, in which blowing a soap bubble is implicitly likened not only to the blowing of glass but also to the painting of an illusionistic picture, whose illusion is as evanescent as the bubble on whose surface the very material colors—the pigments of painting—are deposited. As if to say, contra Diderot, "O Chardin! It *is* white, [pink and blue] that you mix on your palette!" It is the magic of materials that transform themselves into something else altogether, all in front of the rapt eyes of the watchful little boy inside the painting, who mutely mirrors what the viewer does so wordlessly outside and in front of the painting.

CHAPTER TWO

Giorgio Morandi and the Matter of Still Life

The shining, glinting surfaces of highly worked silver and the duller gleam of pewter; the transparency, reflectivity, and refractivity, and also the roundedness, of blown glass, and its tendency to shatter into sharp shards; the limpid, liquid glow of white wine; the foldability of ink-printed paper; the wetness and pearliness of the inside of a couple of rocky-shelled oysters; the pale yellow moisture of a lemon's interior and the pitted opacity of its exterior peel, lined with its soft white pith; the cracking of a bumpy brown walnut; the drape of gray wool cloth over the side of an equally gray stone surface: these are some of the material properties rendered in one of the many grayish-brown, virtually monochromatic breakfast still lifes, or *banketje*, by Willem Claesz. Heda (figure 21), a prime avatar of the so-called Golden Age of Dutch seventeenth-century art, in which the genre of still life figured large.[1] Like its siblings—for Heda painted many similar paintings—this is a still life that uses the medium of oil paint, with its properties of sheen and translucency, to depict a host of materialities other than its own, and thereby to work through the relationship between itself as a material object—an oil painting—and all of the diverse material objects (silver, pewter, glass, wine, paper, oyster, lemon, walnut, wool, stone) that it depicts.

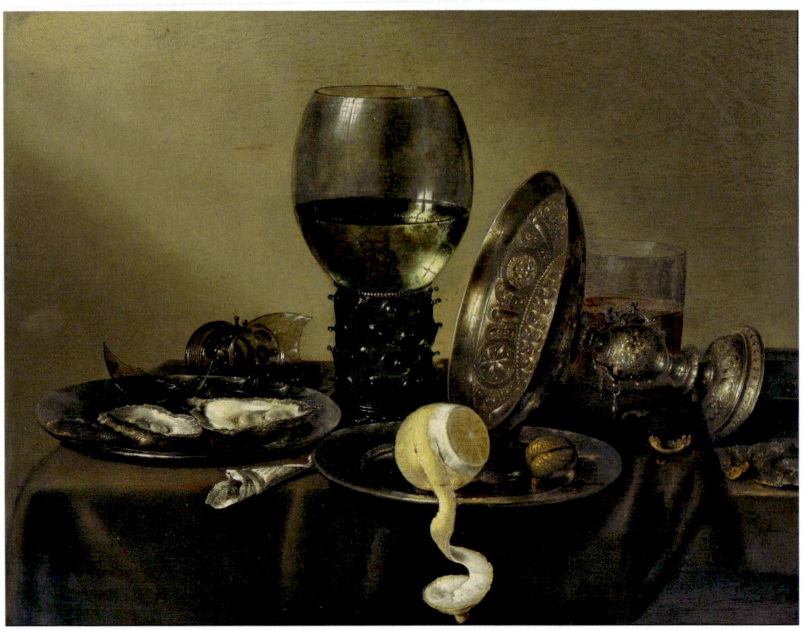

Figure 21. Willem Claesz. Heda, *Still Life with Roemer*, 1634. Oil on canvas. 16 7/8 × 22 3/8 in. (43 × 57 cm). Collection Museum Boijmans Van Beuningen, Rotterdam / Photography: Studio Tromp.

The work of the twentieth-century Italian painter Giorgio Morandi, whose well-known obsession with still life is the focus of this essay, deliberately eschews most of the diverse effects of illusionistic materiality found in the Dutch heyday of the genre, of which the painting by Heda described above is just one example: to begin an essay on Morandi with a brief foray into a work such as Heda's is first of all to juxtapose the illusionistic plenitude of the latter to the absence of the same in the former. Yet there are some notable continuities between one and the other as well: most generally and obviously, the use of oil paint; more particularly, the muted, monochrome palette shared by both; but also the repetitiveness of the still-life genre, the apparently mindless commitment to the mindlessness—the thingness—of things, and most of all, the attention to matter—more than that, the self-reflexive dedication to the mutual imbrication of object matter and painting matter.

It is a habit of mind, particularly in the West, to think that matter is the opposite of mind. In this essay, I want to argue, instead, that painting is a form of material thought, and nowhere more so than in paintings that represent material objects—namely, those that belong to the genre of still life (*stilleven*/*stilleben* in Dutch and German, *nature morte* / *natura morta* in French and Italian, or *bodegón* in Spanish).[2] The lowest on the ladder of the old academic hierarchy of value, still life also has the capacity to be a particularly poignant form of "pensive image" or "meta-painting," as two recent writers have put it—perhaps precisely because of its low status.[3] That is to say, in part, that still life's approach to thought is necessarily a slow and stealthy one. But it is also to say that the genre's lowness, which derives from its involvement with the bodily and the material—as opposed to the association of the high genres of history painting and other figural or human-centered subject matter with mind, thought, and ensoulment—is exactly what qualifies it to "think" materially about its own material status.

The centerpiece of this essay is a late still life by Morandi, to which I turn now, in order to begin to elucidate the ways in which his various refusals of the illusionist possibilities on offer in the European still-life tradition constitute their own kind of material thought about the related thingness of oil painting and the object world it represents. I shall come back to Heda's painting, however, and to a series of excurses on a selective range of pictures of objects that seem to want to think through what it means for a painting to be a material thing in relation to a variety of other material things—before returning to the broader implications of Morandi's reiterative engagement with the apparently most banal and trivial of concerns, the indeterminately scaled landscape of the tabletop and its mute inhabitants.

A STILL LIFE BY GIORGIO MORANDI

Let us look closely at that one small still life, painted in 1956, that hangs together with another still-life painting by Morandi in the Yale University Art Gallery (figure 22). It depicts seven objects that sit and stand together with simple gravity. Simultaneously otherworldly and strangely human, they are grouped very closely together indeed, so that they verge on touching, even when there is a breath of dark space between them. They are abstract in their shapes and yet very concrete, and restrained in their colors, which range from a dull celadon green to a milky navy blue, a chalky off-white, a brownish black, a pallid peach, and a light shade of slightly dirty pinkish taupe, all against a grayish, mushroom-colored background and counter surface. They are determinedly matte; there is neither glistening glass nor glinting metallic surface to interrupt the grayed range of tones that describes this little object world. In short, though its color range is not unlike that of Heda's still life, it couldn't be more different, or more limited in its materiality. In fact, one gets a lot further in listing the material effects *not* present in this late still life by Morandi than in describing those that are. And the same is true of its slightly larger companion piece in the Yale University Art Gallery (figure 23), painted the year before, in 1955, of six similar objects: the same white bottle and two vertical boxes, this time with a cylindrical object behind the peach box, and a pair of smaller bottles to the right, one similarly white, and the other blue and diagonally fluted, and so with just the barest of hints of the surface detail that one might expect from the history of still-life painting.

Earlier on, Morandi had allowed himself moments of gleam and saturated color, in the form of copper pitchers, glinting dark glass bottles, and the occasional bright red or orange vessel. He would now and then continue to include something fluted, or something possessed of a hint of ceramic shine, in his larger arrays of dull colors and plain, matte surfaces, some of them very broadly brushworked, as if to contrast the matte, rough surface of

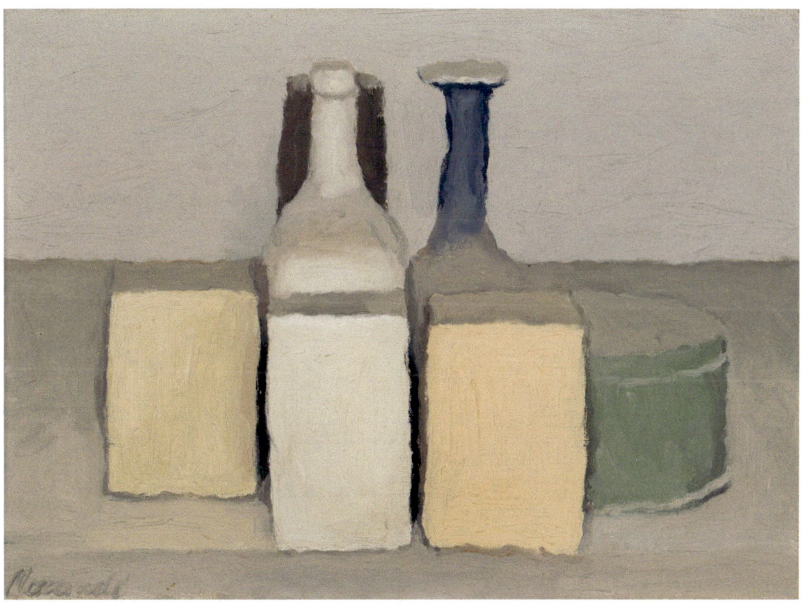

Figure 22. Giorgio Morandi, *Still Life*, 1956. Oil on canvas. 10 × 14 in. (25.2 × 35.2 cm). Yale University Art Gallery, Gift of Mr. and Mrs. Paul Mellon, B.A. 1929 © 2025 Artists Rights Society (ARS), New York / SIAE, Rome.

the painting itself to the occasionally glossy smoothness of the interiors of bowls or the exteriors of bottles, sometimes rendered with strokes of very thick white paint.

But reflectivity of any kind was barred, particularly in the last decade of his work, before he died in 1964 at the age of seventy-four. Transparency and translucency were also ruled out of the spectrum of illusionistic opportunities of which he allowed himself to partake. And there would be no delicate crystal, no figured chinaware, no projecting bone-handled knives, no intricately worked gold or silver, no thick-piled exotic carpets, no patterned tapestries, no white linen, no citrus fruit with pitted skin, no curled peel or visible pulp, no mouthwatering red apples or swelling pears or sliced melons,

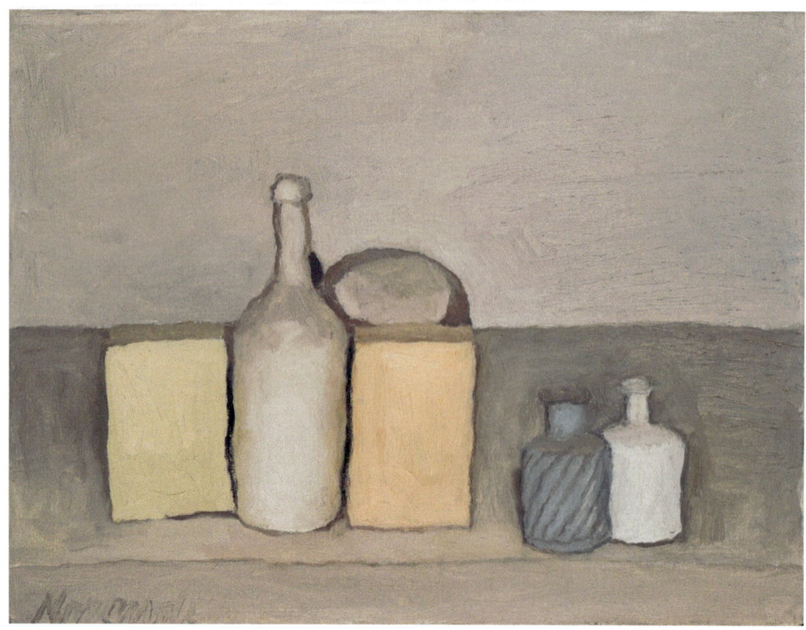

Figure 23. Giorgio Morandi, *Still Life*, 1955. Oil on canvas. 12 × 16 in. (30.5 × 40.8 cm). Yale University Art Gallery, Gift of Mr. and Mrs. Paul Mellon, B.A. 1929 © 2024 Artists Rights Society (ARS), New York / SIAE, Rome.

no leafy vegetables, no viscous fish flesh, no glowing liquid. Instead, the same dull, dusty things were repeated over and over again, and in the 1950s the range became even more restricted than it had been before: a copper pitcher shoved in the back so its gleam cannot be seen; occasionally an odd funnel-topped vessel; matte white bottles again and again; sometimes a dark or a light blue or a pale yellow or a brick-colored one; two or more dark cylinders or rectangular blocks; tin canisters and paper and cardboard boxes, including the same two that appear in the Yale still life; occasionally a blue-striped white jar. Most frequently, his objects are seen head-on, more or less at eye level, with few cast shadows, and little to no sense of either perspectival foreshortening or the larger tabletop world on which they are situated—though there are, here and there, some exceptions that prove that rule. The only other variation he allowed himself was by means of facture or paint handling, format, and the overall tint of the restrained palette and background hue, ranging between pinkish beige, pale olive, and blue-tinged gray.[4]

In 1956, perhaps more than ever, Morandi liked to stress his reticences and restrictions by means of repetition: often the very same objects, give or take one or two items, set in differently shaped canvases—more or less square and thus somewhat constricted (figure 24), or in even longer rectangles that allowed more room on the sides so that their spaces feel a bit more open and relaxed. Just as he ground and mixed his own pigments, so Morandi also either stretched, prepared, and primed his own canvases or had them custom-made, which means that the relationship of his compositions of simple objects to the shape and edges of those canvases was a considered one. And he carefully plotted the placement of his objects, as is demonstrated by the overlapping pencil marks on the paper "ground plan" that he devised (figure 25).[5] Thus, that the celadon-colored cylindrical box lines right up with the right edge of the almost-square canvas, and that it is given much more breathing room in the more spacious rectangular canvas, allowing us to see that the darker gray along the lower edge (which is merely hinted at in the Yale canvas) constitutes the lip of the table as it abuts the front plane of the picture, were all carefully calculated decisions. Just as was the doubling of the dark vertical vase in the back of both, along with the removal of the blue-necked bottle and its replacement by a shorter, pallid half-cylindrical form in the center right of the more expansive canvas. Not to mention the use of the dark vertical vase forms to confound the distinction between object and background, or the tiny hint of a projecting base emerging from just behind the yellowish box on the left of both. Or the way the top of that same pale yellow box on the left of the Yale painting lines right up with the back edge of the table top, where it meets the vertical wall,

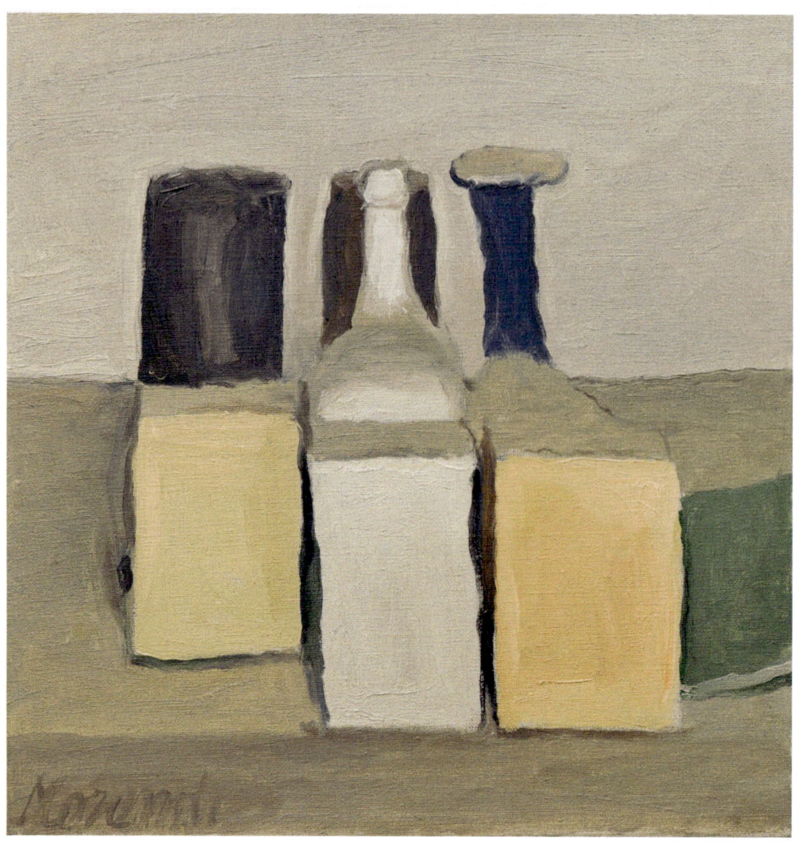

Figure 24. Giorgio Morandi, *Still Life*, 1956. Oil on canvas. 13¾ × 14 in. (35.8 × 35.2 cm). Museo Morandi, Bologna. © 2025 Artists Rights Society (ARS), New York / SIAE, Rome.

so that it is confounded with that rear horizon. Or finally, the way the lip of the white bottle lines right up with the top of the dark vase behind it, an effect doubled and tripled in other compositions.

Before depicting them in paint, Morandi applied gesso to many of the glass bottles that posed for him (as seen in the beautiful photographs made by Joel Meyerowitz of individual items posed on the penciled paper ground

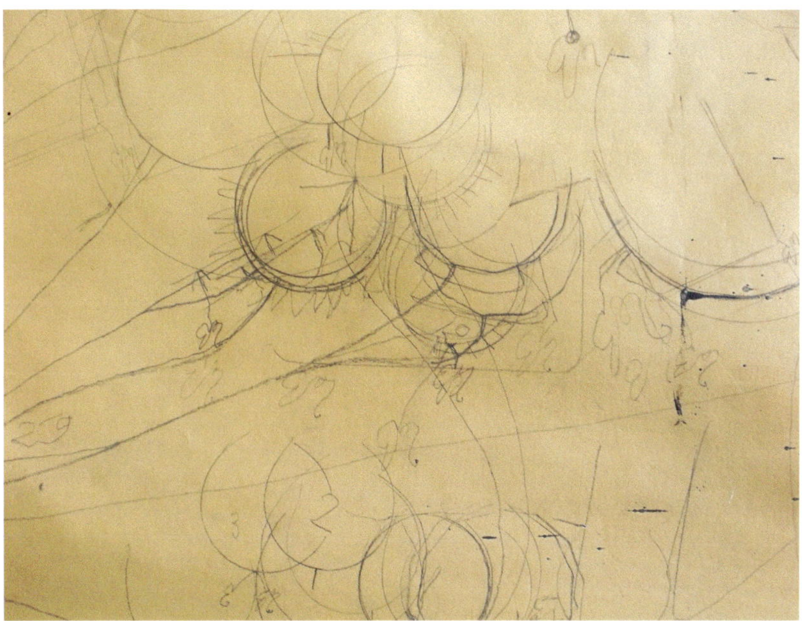

Figure 25. Giorgio Morandi, *Foglio con tracce di disegno per la collocazione degli oggetti*, detail, n.d. Pencil on paper. 32 1/2 × 35 3/4 in. (82.5 × 91 cm). Museo Morandi, Bologna. © 2025 Artists Rights Society (ARS), New York / SIAE, Rome.

plan in Morandi's studio, figure 26), which suggests that he was also quite deliberate in avoiding sheen and shine, the bright white highlight and the bit of reflection, the punctuation by color and luster and texture and detail.[6] He filled other glass vessels with pigment or painted on them, and he was insistent that all of the objects positioned on the three tables, set at three different heights in his studio, should accrue dust.[7] Thus it is evident that he was quite purposeful in his avoidance of the inventorying not only of the different materialities of glass and metal, porcelain, fabric, fruit, fish, wine, and so on, but also of paint's capacity to render and replace those materialities that had marked the earlier European history of the still-life genre, as far

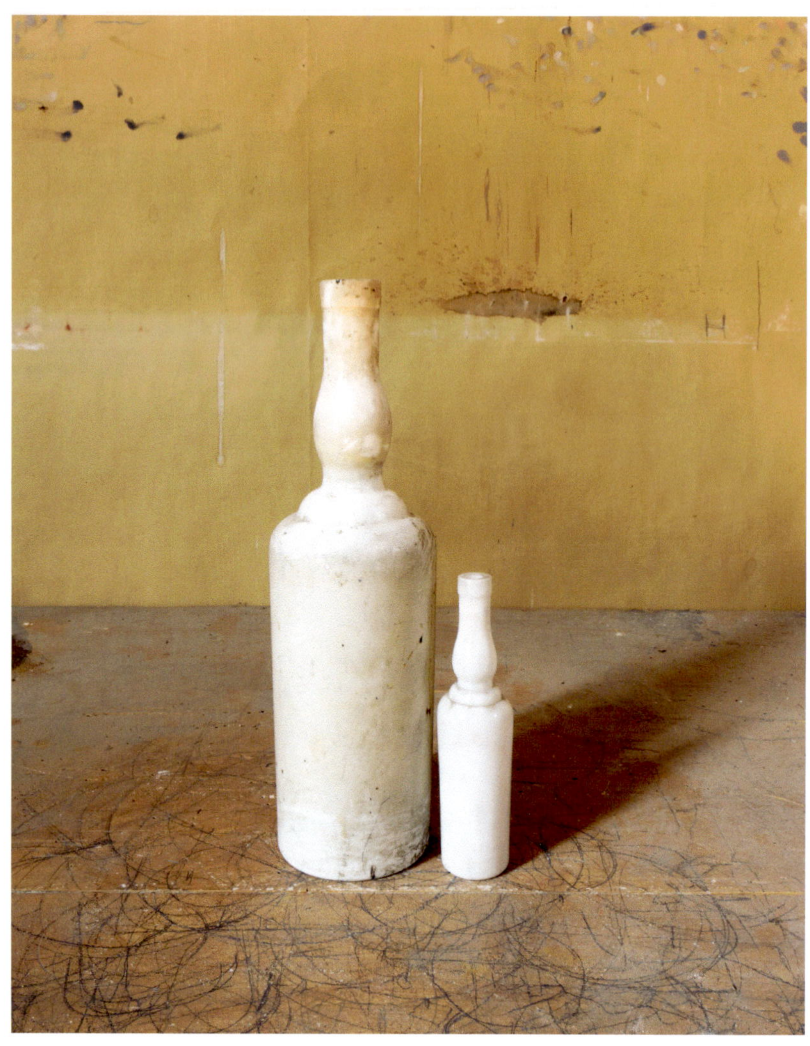

Figure 26. Joel Meyerowitz, *Morandi's Objects*, 69: *White Bottles*, 2015. ©Joel Meyerowitz, Courtesy of Howard Greenberg Gallery.

back as Pompeian "rhopography," meaning, in ancient Greek, the depiction of trivial things.[8] In fact, Morandi's matte, plaster-like tonality seems to reach back to those bits of Vesuvian villa fresco and, indeed, to the Roman refining of the materials of cement and concrete. But even in those early wall paintings, ancient Roman painters had been fascinated with trying to render the transparency of the glass artifacts that were one of the high points of their culture's array of artisanal inventions. The avoidance of that fascination, one shown to advantage later in the glossy medium of oil paint, was one of Morandi's principal austerities.

How can we make sense of Morandi's abstinences? Of the deliberateness of putting gesso on his glass bottles before he depicted them in his canvases? And of his stressing of other aspects of oil paint besides the glossiness of its medium, and its ability to be ever more diluted in layers of glassy glaze? Both that deliberateness and that emphasis are self-reflexive, for to paint gesso or to apply pigments directly onto the actual bottles in his studio was to ensure that their surfaces would be the equivalents of the prepared ground of painting before it is painted. To emphasize the similarity of oil paint to mediums like plaster and cement was also to turn the still-life world back to its ground, and to elide it with the surfaces of walls on which paintings hang. To stress the slippery, slathery manipulability of his matte pigments, rather than their glossiness, was to underline the materiality of his medium and its simple pleasures, rather than the gourmand delights of illusionism that that medium makes possible. And to choose paper and cardboard and cheap tin boxes as prime among the objects to paint into his still-life paintings was to do something akin to what Josef Albers did around the same time, in recommending that his students at Yale carry out their color exercises with cut pieces of matte paper so as to eliminate the distraction of textural variability.[9] In this way as well, Morandi chose to circle back around to the plane surface on which he was painting and which his rectangular boxes face so directly, such that they are exactly flush with it, aligning their paint-on-paper, -cardboard, or -metal flatness with the paint-on-canvas flatness of the painting that they inhabit.

Yet all this with a difference from, say, the abstractionist moves of Piet Mondrian, in 1912, abstracting cubistically from Cézanne to arrive at the bare lineaments of a ginger jar caught up in a faceted grid from which almost all detail has been leached. Or of Henri Matisse, in 1915, abstracting from the rich plenitude and luxurious *pronkstilleven* illusionism of seventeenth-century Dutch painter Jan Davidz. De Heem to arrive at a flattened-out array of vivid color areas reducing fruit bowl, ewers, glassware, and musical instruments to an obviously drawn and painted surface arrangement that plainly spells out its own two-dimensional planarity. Mondrian's and Matisse's still-life moves were exactly the sort of thing described in a general way by Clement Greenberg in his famous account of the emergence of abstraction out of late nineteenth-century naturalism, as painting being "hunted back to its medium," as he put it.[10]

Morandi, by contrast, insisted on the tangible reality of his abstracted things, as is attested by the gessoing and painting of his bottles even before he depicted them. And the double act of painting the thing that he would then paint again, of applying off-white oil paint with glue and gypsum in it to the object that he was about to paint into a picture, or of painting pigment directly onto its surface, was a strangely contradictory inversion of the usual direction of abstraction, with its move away from representing objects in the world. It was to try to make his objects conform to the material logic of painting in advance, and thus, rather than moving altogether away from outward reference to objects, allowing for a cautious turn back to the physical reality of the world to which those objects belonged. Except that that outward reference to the real world was peculiarly inward at the same time, for it was enclosed in the tight circle of painting's reality, the medium's physicality. At the same time, Morandi's particular brand of abstract realism yielded a quiet opening up of still life's, not to mention abstraction's, allusiveness, just as his asceticism allowed for a controlled and very discrete kind of voluptuousness.

Both characteristics of Morandi's hermetic brand of still-life painting are demonstrated in the little 1956 picture that is this essay's centerpiece. To take the question of its allusiveness first, we might think of it in relation to a figure much admired by Morandi, Paul Cézanne, whose still-life paintings suggest landscapes and human figures, not to mention an animacy, even an eroticism, that is noticeably lacking in his portraits of people and his renderings of the nude female body.[11] Something similar, and yet different, happens in Morandi's painting, but with extreme tact. Two parental figures seem to be surrounded by their family, standing while their offspring sit. Although the gessoed white bottle, to the left, might be ensconced in a high-backed chair, as the solid father of the group with his slenderer partner standing next to him, pulling just a little away from him, at the same time the brown-black shape behind the white bottle looms like the spectral shadow of an ancestor. Alternatively, a cityscape with tapering skyscrapers and stolid apartment towers presents itself on the tabletop, constructed out of so many building blocks. Or a geological landscape of differently shaped boulders and dolmens is proposed, perhaps.[12] The words *chasm* and *megalith* come to mind, despite the modest scale of the painting. Indeed, the little picture has an odd scalelessness that allows for the diminutive to mushroom, Alice-in-Wonderland style, into the outsize in the imagination, and then back down again to the proportions of things to hand.[13] In short, the little that is there can conjure up a lot in the imagination.

With regard to the second question—that of the sensuous appeal of Morandi's practice—adjectives often used to describe the application of paint, like *buttery*, seem to morph from the metaphoric almost into the literal in the face of his small painting, in which everything seems to face us, and face off against us, with the toothsome, tactile materiality of its paintedness. And the evocativeness of colors also goes to work. Because the bottle on the left is milk-white, it might be a milk bottle. Because the bottle on the right has a blued neck, it has the blues. Because the green half-cylinder container to the right is the green of celadon, it hovers between paper and ceramic. Because the colors of cream and peach and chalk and mushroom are used, peaches and cream become laden with the taste and feel of calcium and fungus. Because the whites are a bit dishwatery, soil and dust inflect the canvas. And because the background is the color of cement, it implies a concrete surface, not to mention the fact that the plastering of paint suggests plaster, while the evocation of concrete aligns with the concreteness of the depiction of concrete things. In short, the discrete sensuality of this work rests on its quiet combination of the allusive and the material dimensions of still-life painting, at both the optical and the haptic, the literal and the figurative levels.

Nevertheless, there is a lot less to describe directly in this still life than in most of the rest of the history of still-life painting, with the genre's attachment to illusionism, and the transformation, which that illusionism solicits, of the detached desires of the eye into the more visceral hungers of the body. In Morandi's little still life, assiduous attention finds its limits pretty quickly, and must linger on effects of facture and relationship, rather than the textural differentiation of the specific things represented. So the eye begins to note the traces of the painting hand, such as the movement from the vertical to the horizontal direction of the brush in the peach box to the right, or the looping slur of paint in the paler box to the left, or the swoop and swirl of cement color, suggesting a brisker flick of the wrist, in the portion of the background wall near the left horizon of the tabletop, all in monochrome areas that defy immediate notice. Our eyes register as well the graying of the part of the milk-white bottle that narrows toward the neck, as well as the bluing of the adjacent bottle's neck as it rises up out of its slate-smeared body. And then we take in the wavering of the edges of the bottle's neck, the unsteady overlay of a milkier blue on a darker blue, the skewing of one contour and the wobbliness of the other, just where the expanse of wall seems to eat into it at the moment of its downward swell, on the right, into its indeterminate, gray-brown body.

Rather than traits of the objects depicted, standing before us in the present tense, these are markers of the past movements of the hand, as the painter struggled with the eye-hand coordination of the painting act. Or to put it differently, they are indexical marks that refer not outward to the objects represented but inward, to the physical act of painting.[14] Or rather, not to the nouns—this object or that object, bottle or box—but to the verb of painting. And it is there that Morandi seems to have found his muted pleasure, in the delicate eroticism of the physical manipulability of paint, its slipping and sliding over the tactile surface, even as the viewing eye feels the painter trying rigorously to get it right. This is as far as can be from the voluptuary caress of a painterly painter like Rubens or Renoir, and yet it is here that one understands best why the gesture of the brush is called a "stroke." And it is here, too, because so much else is stripped away, that one confronts the regressive umami of the lipid materiality of oil paint.

It is worth noticing one other effect of the movement of Morandi's hand on and in the coloristically restrained surface of his canvas, whose weave is often visible, especially around the edges of things. That is the quality of dense depth that emerges from the impenetrable interstices between his vertical boxes: impossible to describe that feeling of obscure fathomlessness that is the result of the combined darkness and thinness of the divide between things, so that each fissure becomes a little abyss, created by the simple motion of the black-laden brush. And from there the eye is led to the mind's awareness of the impossible closeness of these things to each other, of there being no room for them, really, as small as they are, on and in this cramped surface world with its incalculable space, which is contained by its frame while seeming to stretch to horizontal infinity. Where is there space for that dark brown object behind the milky bottle? Where is there space for that bottle between the object behind it and the white box in front of it?

Where is there room for the blue-necked bottle, and exactly where does it stand relative to its milk-white companion, and the pale peach box in front of it? Precisely how wide or narrow, deep or shallow, are the grayed tops of those boxes, especially the one on the left whose uppermost edge is all but indistinguishable from the leftward tabletop horizon? And what exactly is the extent and shape of the curved celadon box to the right, which is so barely distinguished by the hand of the painter wielding his cement-colored brush from the ground of the painting? Not to mention those thin lines that edge the top and bottom of the pale green semicylinder at right: where, exactly, do they begin and end? That none of these questions are answerable speaks to the qualitative ambiguity of this world of still-life painting.

At the same time, it speaks to the existentialism of the business of representational painting that Morandi's work puts front and center stage. More than the confrontation with the passing of time and the attendant mortality and entropy of all things that was often suggested in earlier still lifes, I would argue that the poignance of a still life like Morandi's is that it sets up an encounter with the otherness of the world, its existence as that which is *not me*, which is outside of me, I the subject of the encounter. It does so more insistently than even the portrait, which takes the likeness of other people, or the self for that matter, as its charge and brief. Whereas in that case we at least know what it feels like to be a person—maybe not *that* person, but we do know what it feels like to be some particular person—we do not know what it feels like to be a thing. And Morandi's peculiar life of work in the genre performs that encounter persistently. Over and over again he faced off against that which was not him, and asked it to face off, however blankly, against him. Over and over again he took the task of representation as the task of doing just that, not by pretended or solicited possession or incorporation, as in all the delights of foodstuffs or luxury goods presented to the eye by the illusionistic still life, but through the hesitations of the hand trying to adjudicate what the eye sees outside of and beyond its enclosure in the self's body, and to bring it all home by rendering it and therefore making it real, on the canvas, in an in-between zone between the self and the world. Morandi's most often quoted remark was that "nothing is more abstract than reality," thus speaking to an essential bond between abstraction and the realism of still life.[15] If there was an incipient abstraction in still life's realism from the beginning, Morandi brought it to the fore by stripping away all but the structural relation, both physical and psychical, between the "I" and the "it." All else is eliminated; the rest of the world is blocked out, so as to focus on that very basic question.[16]

NINE EXCURSUSES INTO THE HISTORY OF STILL-LIFE PAINTING

Excursus 1: Michelangelo Merisi da Caravaggio

Morandi's obsession with still life necessarily engaged with the history of the genre, even in disavowing such a lot of what it had to offer. And more broadly, his was a painting practice much concerned with the history of art writ large—indeed, many have been the arguments as to whether he was an Italian traditionalist or an Italian modernist, or somehow both.[17] His admirations included not only Cézanne in the French modernist tradition, but also the so-called Italian "Primitives": among them, Giotto, Masaccio, and Piero della Francesca, whose simplified fresco styles find their echo in Morandi's matte, mute objects.[18] And he is reported to have had a special interest in the work of Caravaggio—most of which, of course, belongs not to the genre of still life but to the figural genres at the top of the academic hierarchy—namely, the narrative scenes, the religious and mythological subjects, that formed the most prestigious crux of Italy's earlier history of painting.[19] Whether or not Morandi was interested in Caravaggio's famous contender for first freestanding easel painting with the subject matter of still life, and still life alone, with no narrative or other motive for painting it, I do not know—though certainly he did travel to Milan, where the *Basket of Fruit*

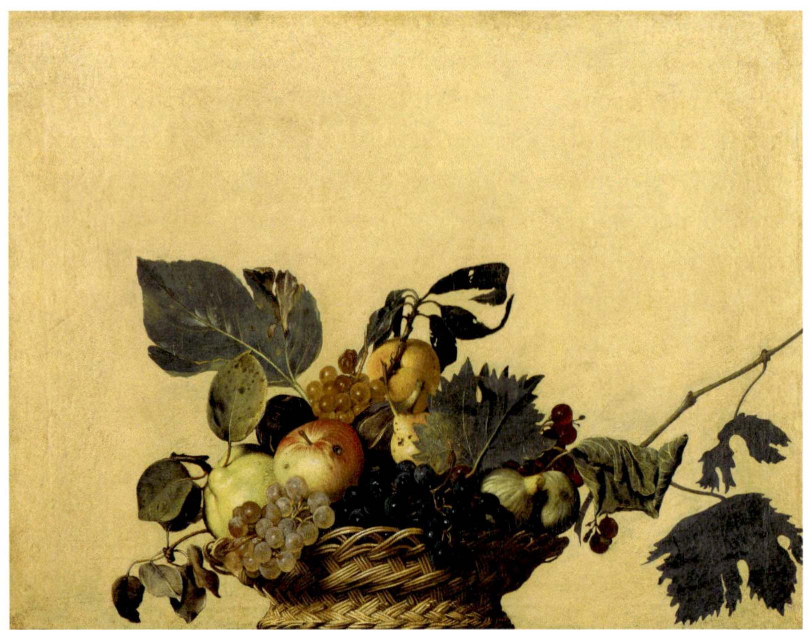

Figure 27. Michelangelo Merisi da Caravaggio, *Still Life with Fruit*, ca. 1599. Oil on canvas. 18 × 25 3/8 in. (46 × 64.5 cm). Biblioteca Ambrosiana, Milan.

of 1599 (figure 27) has resided in the Biblioteca Ambrosiana since the seventeenth century. That is the little painting that is the focus of my first excursus into the history of still-life painting.[20]

Appearing to sit on the brink of a narrow ledge against a wall, Caravaggio's *Basket of Fruit* seems to reach back to the Roman beginnings of Italian wall-fresco painting, and in particular to the still lifes executed in that medium (such as a *Basket of Figs* in the Villa Poppaea in Oplontis from the first century CE). Painted on canvas, it looks as if it's painted on the wall. For all the precise textural realism of the basket weave, the translucent grapes, the shiny lemon, the blemished apple, the wizened figs, and differently shaped fig and apple and grape leaves, the flattened silhouettes of the two rightmost grape leaves play off against the rest, particularly against the wrinkled grape leaf next to them, as well as against the material evocation of a plaster wall, to point back to their own status as paint-made shape on a surface. Is it wall or canvas? Is it paint, or paper-thin leaf, or cast shadow? Is it real or figment? Does it project or recede in space, or is it flat? And then, is the ledge on which it sits some sort of horizontal surface, whether wood or stone, perpendicular to the wall, or simply the framing bottom edge of the painting?

Here, in short, is a still-life painting that, right at the outset of the genre, meditates on its own material properties, in this case its own oil medium as a substitute for fresco, its own easel-picture status as a simulacrum of the flat wall on which it hangs—less as a disembodied two-dimensional plane than as a real, textured, touchable surface that degrades over time, just as the red-yellow apple acquires its bruise and the grape leaf crumples as it desiccates. The glints on the leftmost grape leaf and on the two bunches of green grapes cascading below it; the lemon-yellow lemon with its pitted skin on the one side of the composition versus the creased casings of the gray-green figs on the other side of it; the dense weave of the straw-colored basket; the cropped bit of grapevine twig at right; and the shadow-casting of various kinds, at once modeling and flattening the basket and the fruit within it: together, these amount to highly successful illusionistic devices, afforded by the material properties of oil-suspended pigment, with its own glisten and gleam, which are at the same time playfully self-questioning.[21] In short, Caravaggio's *Basket of Fruit* set the stage for one kind of materialized pictorial thinking about the relationship between the matter of painting and that of its depicted objects, encoding that material thought into the DNA of still-life painting.

Excursus 2: Juan Sánchez Cotán

A few years later, in 1602 or so, a Spaniard by the name of Juan Sánchez Cotán painted what the Spanish call a *bodegón*—named after the pantry

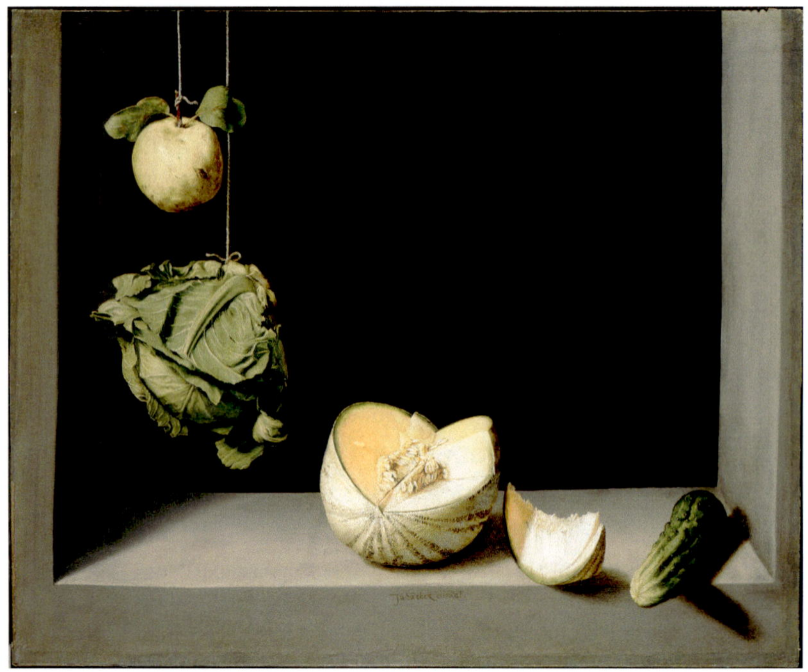

Figure 28. Juan Sánchez Cotán, *Still Life with Quince, Cabbage, Melon, and Cucumber*, ca. 1602. Oil on canvas, 27 1/8 in. × 33 1/4 in. (68.9 × 84.5 cm). The San Diego Museum of Art: Gift of Anne R. and Amy Putnam, 1945.43. www.sdmart.org.

in which foodstuffs were kept—that sits at the ascetic end of the still-life spectrum and presently resides in the San Diego Museum of Art (figure 28).[22] Concerned with fruit and vegetable matter—a quince, a cabbage, a melon, a melon slice, and a cucumber, hanging and sitting together in a dark, cool niche to stave off their rotting—this still life preserves its organic items forever. Yet the contusion on the side of the quince and the seed on the sharply sliced interior flesh of the cut melon, looking, at least to me, a bit like the tear on the cheek of a human martyr, both allude to the mortality, intertwined with the fertility, of fruit-bearing plant life.

Simple food necessary for sustenance, the things depicted in this painting are contrasted not only to each other—a set of leafed and pulpy roundnesses, ranging from hard, smooth exterior to soft interior, that give way to the elongated, uneven surface and shape of the cucumber at right—but also to the mineral hardness of the stone surface on which some of them rest, and the black nothingness against which they are seen. They are assigned properties of weight and balance, restfulness and stasis, that belong to the physics of shadow-casting, gravity-bound substance and mass, while also suggesting a contemplative mood, even a state of meditation. At the same time, they propose an affinity with the cosmic realm of astronomical bodies and with the abstractions of geometry, as if wanting us to consider the relations among mathematics, hard minerality, and soft, biomorphic materiality, all in a chiaroscural, oil-on-canvas, almost square rectangle. In short, if a still life can close the distance between immeasurable infinity and measurable finitude, nothing and something, mysticism and matter, human thinking and inhuman stuff, this is the one that does it.

On the face of it, the somewhat later still-life paintings of Francisco de Zurbaran, such as the famous *Still Life with Lemons, Oranges, and a Rose* of 1632, or better still, the *Still Life with Pots* of 1650 in the Prado (figure 29), might seem more suited to a juxtaposition with Morandi's work: for all the difference of their dark, chiaroscuro-bound mystery, the separate side-by-side-ness and shallow frontality of their objects and object groupings might be seen to foreshadow the similar facingness and simple dignity of Morandi's bottles and pitchers, boxes and canisters. And their focus on hard metal and ceramic is more in line with Morandi's later insistence on human-made receptacles rather than on Nature's perishable produce. Indeed, both the white highlights on three of the four vessels in the *Still Life with Pots*—two of them as white as any of Morandi's gessoed bottles—and the subtle anthropomorphics of their handles-on-hips stances make me think forward to our twentieth-century Bolognese painter. But Cotán's *bodegón* interests me more

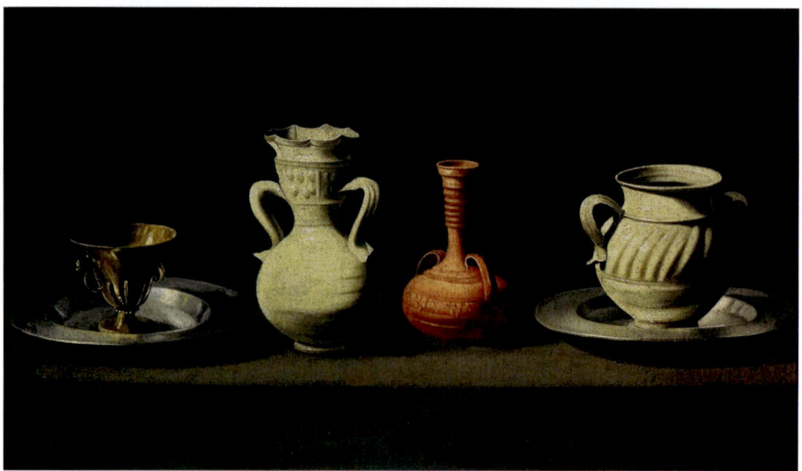

Figure 29. Francisco de Zurbaran, *Still Life with Pots*, 1650. Oil on canvas. 18 × 33 in. (46 × 84 cm). Prado, Madrid. © Photographic Archive Museo Nacional del Prado.

in this context, partly because of its humble austerity and its scale-defying indeterminacy, but even more because it exudes a thoughtfulness about the relation between matter and spirit—between the most unassuming of material things in the here and now and a dematerialized beyond.

Excursus 3: Willem Kalf

Another seventeenth-century painting sits at the luxury end of the still-life spectrum: *pronkstilleven*, it was called. This is the Dutch master Willem Kalf's *Still Life with Nautilus Cup* of 1662, presently in the Thyssen-Bornemisza Museum in Madrid (figure 30). Even more than in the painting by Heda discussed at the beginning, here we see the full use of oil paint's capacities for sheen, shine, gleam, and glaze, deployed to render the most expensive objects of the Dutch trade in luxury goods: in addition to the nautilus cup itself, fine Venetian glass, the wine within it, the intricately worked porcelain bowl, the invisible sugar within it—sweet to the lemon's sour—a silver

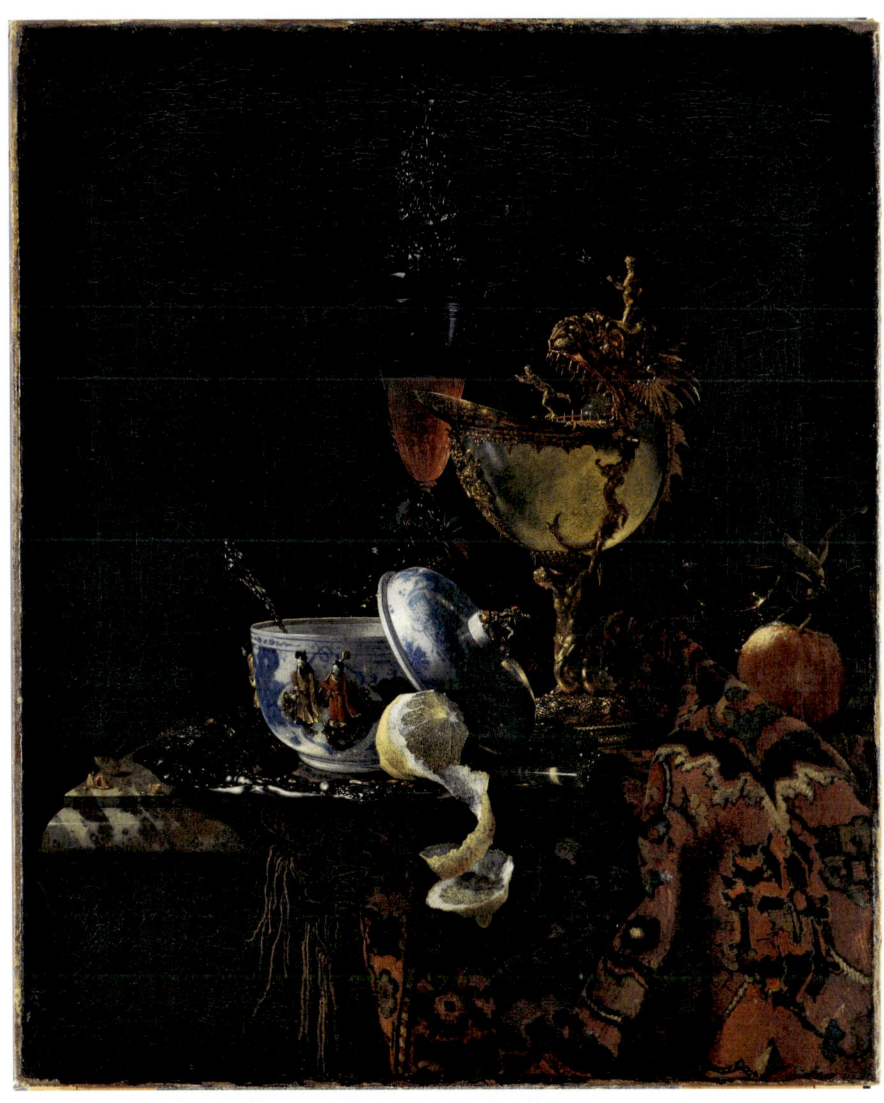

Figure 30. Willem Kalf, *Still Life with Chinese Bowl, Nautilus Cup and Other Objects*, 1662. Oil on canvas. 31 × 26 in. (79 × 67 cm). Museo Nacional Thyssen-Bornemisza, Madrid. Inv. no. 203 (1962.10). © Museo Nacional Thyssen-Bornemisza, Madrid.

spoon and plate, a marble-topped table, and again, little bits of walnut detritus, a Turkish carpet, a projecting bone-handled knife. In this case, the painter pits his skills and his medium against those of the artisan: the glassblower, the ceramicist—potter, glazer, and porcelain painter—the weaver, the silver- and goldsmith. And in so doing he seems to have ruminated not only about the relation between the values of raw and worked materials, of materiality and skill, of the literal and illusionistic—the gold standard of actual gold versus depicted gold, possibly using the basest and yet among the most expensive of paint materials, so-called Indian yellow, made with cow's urine, versus what we might call a kind of optical gold, the reflective glint of yellow light on a smooth, translucent surface.[23]

Kalf also seems to have been thinking about the relation between Nature and Culture, the artifices of God the Great Artificer and of the human maker. For that, of course, is what the nautilus cup itself is all about: the goldsmith vying with and trumping the original artistry of the nautilus shell, polished to a very high sheen.[24] And it is what the rest of the still life concerns itself with as well: materials like wool that is shorn from the sheep, clay and minerals that come out of the ground, the shell that comes from the sea, the glass that derives from sand, and the fruit and nut that falls or is picked from the tree—hence the bit of leaf and stem attached to the clementine or orange over on the far right—all removed or uprooted by shearing, mining, harvest, and trade, and transformed into something else by human fabrication.[25] And that is what Kalf's picture demonstrates itself to be as well: a bravura performance in transforming paint materials into painted illusions, producing the magicianship of a mirage that emerges into sight and then disappears again into invisibility, all out of the flat black of the painting's ground.

Kalf's painting ups the ante on both the inventorying of luxury objects and the illusionistic skills of Heda's still life (figure 21). Where Heda's "fijn schilderij" style of highly detailed, shinily glazed-over painting seeks to hide the evidence of the painter's hand, Kalf's more impressionistic handling thematizes the translation of the variety of surfaces that it represents into oil paint, and the transformation of light into colored pigment: the facturing of its opticality. For its highlights in particular—from the white area on the orange fruit at the far right, to the pith of the half-unpeeled lemon, to the ephemeral glints that just barely suggest the intricate working of the flute glass in the uppermost register of the painting as it all but disappears into the darkness that engulfs it—all play much more explicitly at the boundary between paint, light, and the illusion of differently artificed surfaces. Some three centuries later, Morandi would have no truck with either the luxury goods or the illusionistic bravura of Kalf's world of still-life painting, but once in a while he would condense the factural play between white paint and bright highlight into simple strokes of thick white impasto for all to see.

Excursus 4: Cornelius Norbertus Gijsbrechts

In fact, the Dutch and the Flemish seem to have been particularly alive to painting's game of the illusionism of materials, producing genre paintings like Jan Vermeer's *Girl Reading a Letter at an Open Window* (1657–59) in Dresden, where a trompe l'oeil curtain appears to be hung over the painting (right next to a foreground still life), or the 1658 still life by Adriaen van der Spelt, in the Art Institute of Chicago, that insists on the paintedness of its painted illusion by means of a similarly fictive curtain likewise appearing to hang on a curtain rod, this time over the painting of a flower garland, thus pointing both to the material objecthood and to the fakery of the painted thing. But it has its cake and eats it too, because the illusionism of both painted flowers and the shimmer of the painted fabric of the creased and wrinkled satin curtain is so powerful. Again it is the material properties of oil paint and glaze that make that illusionism possible.

And then there is the marvelous *trompe l'oeil* painting by the Flemish Cornelius Gijsbrechts, court painter to the Danish royal family, in the

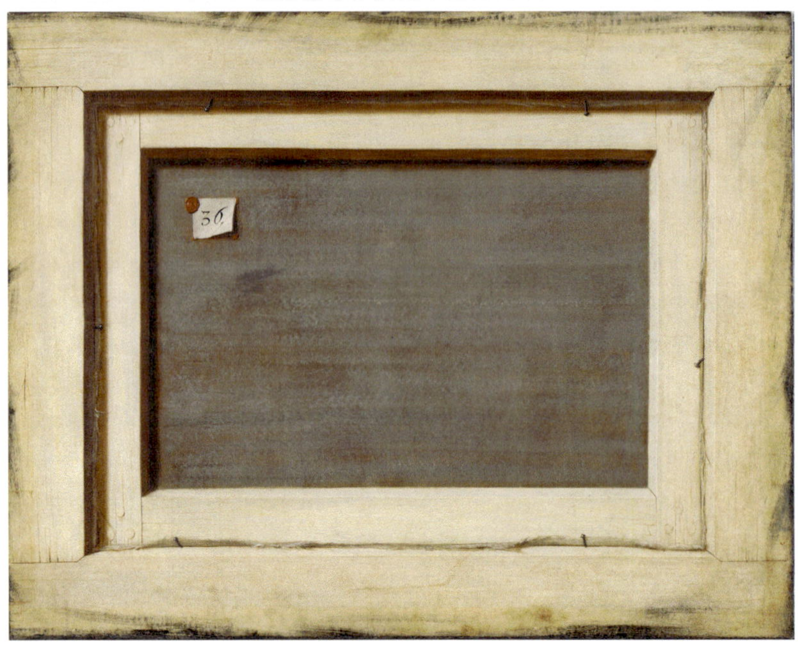

Figure 31. Cornelius Gijsbrechts, *The Reverse Side of a Painting*, 1670. Oil on canvas. 26 1/8 × 34 1/4 in. (66.4 × 87 cm). Statens Museum for Kunst, Copenhagen.

National Gallery of Denmark in Copenhagen, the 1670 *Reverse Side of a Painting* (figure 31).[26] Gijsbrechts's paintings almost always occupied the register of still life, though this one may seem a bit eccentric to the genre, for rather than rendering discrete still life objects sitting on tables or ledges in the represented real world, it renders the back of itself: its dedication to the world of things and their materiality is thus explicitly bent back around to address the painting's own thingness. Its self-reflexive illusionism includes the grain of the wood stretcher, the thready bits of raw canvas stretched through and between the wood, the nails and pins hammered into the wood to hold it together and keep the canvas in it, the traces of paint on the wood—real paint on the fake wood—presumably trailed from the front of the canvas, which is now to be imagined as the back of the canvas, and even the little paper tag on the upper left with the price or inventory number, which once more we might imagine to be the price or inventory number of *this* painting. How could a painter be more clear, through the play of illusionism, that he knew his painting to be a material thing, was thinking about that, and was asking his viewers to think about it too?

Gijsbrechts made painting after painting of a wooden wall of his studio space, with faux paintings of still-life and other subjects seen as if tacked up to the wall, and his painting paraphernalia displayed along with them, including palette, paintbrushes, paint box, and bottles of linseed oil. Indeed, he even went so far as to produce a cutout panel, called a *chantourné*, depicting his easel, the back of a canvas, and all the items just mentioned on a life-size scale. It was as if he wished not only to confuse the eye even more, by undermining the difference between flat and three-dimensional objects, but also to say: these are the materials, tools, and skills that painting is made of, just as the objects that still-life painting depicts are made of materials, by tools, and with skills, though of course they are different ones. And thus, Gijsbrechts's *Reverse Side of a Painting* qualifies not only as a still-life painting concerned with its own materiality as a made thing among and in relation to other made things, but also and therefore as the centerpiece of these excurses into the history of the genre. Having never traveled to Copenhagen, and unlikely to have ever seen a reproduction of this painting, Morandi would not have known of it. Yet I believe it can stand as the obverse of his own peculiar brand of still-life self-reflexivity, predicated as it was on the gessoing and painting of his actual glass bottles and other still-life objects before he painted them into his canvases.

Excursus 5: Jean-Baptiste-Siméon Chardin

I turn now to the quintessential still-life painting of the French eighteenth century, to Jean-Baptiste-Siméon Chardin, and to a different aspect of still-life thought about materiality. In 1728 Chardin made his debut and was accepted into the Royal Academy of Painting and Sculpture in Paris with two large demonstration pieces, both of them now housed in the Louvre: one of them a kitchen piece, the famous *Ray* with its rearing cat, and the other a banquet with a dog who threatens to bring down a mounded pyramid of fruit. These pendant paintings began the painter's lifelong meditation on the relation between the living (the cat and the dog) and the dead (in French, still life is called *nature morte*, or dead nature) as well as between what Claude Lévi-Strauss called "the raw and the cooked."[27] At the same time, they also address the two ends of the food chain of cooking and eating: on the one hand, a meal, its ingredients and its tools, in the process of being assembled, before it is cooked and while its elements are all still in an abjectly raw state, eliciting disgust as well as pleasure; and on the other hand, the tail end of a meal, a highly artificed aristocratic dessert apparently in the process of being consumed. And so, given this theme, perhaps it is also useful to point out that in French, a painting's blended pigments and paint surface was often called a "sauce."

Around the same time and in the years immediately following, Chardin kept on at the theme of the live and the dead, the raw and the cooked, including a series of hunt pictures featuring a dead rabbit and braces of pheasant or pigeon. One painting, in the Metropolitan Museum of Art in New York (figure 32), also relatively large for a still life, puts both rabbit and pigeon together with another cat, crouching and ready to spring, with a silver soup tureen, and fruit and vegetables, including a difficult-to-see stem of leek or celery that arcs dimly over the back of the rabbit. Because of the inclusion of the cat, the hunter and the hunted, not to mention the domestic and the wild, are jammed together. Because of the inclusion of the soup tureen, hunting and cooking, as well as the rawly animal and the highly artificed, are also jammed together. At the same time, there is a conflating, in places, of blood and pigment, seen most disturbingly in the congealing

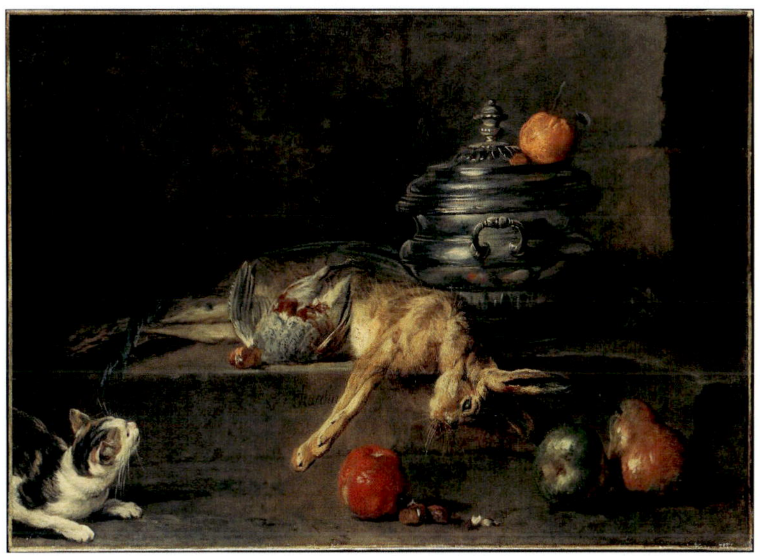

Figure 32. Jean-Baptiste-Siméon Chardin, *The Silver Tureen*, 1728–30. Oil on canvas. 30 × 42½ in. (78.2 × 108 cm). Metropolitan Museum of Art, NY.

drop of red that hangs off the nose and whiskers of the rabbit: a conflation that contends with the optical effect of reflections, seen both fore and aft on the silver surface of the tureen, in which orange, rabbit, red apple, and pear are seen twice, first as depicted objects, and second as patches of color—the very patches of color of which those depicted objects are made. And thus the painting uses the silver tureen and its reflective effects to consider the relation between the visceral and the optical, the carnal and the disembodied, the pitiful and the beautiful, object and paint material.

Though the hunt motif eventually all but disappeared, and his still-life pictures got smaller and smaller, as well as more repetitive, while the aristocratic mound of fruit with which he began diminished to modest, plain little groupings of fruit and single pieces of silver or glassware that dispensed with courtly ostentatiousness in favor of artisan-class simplicity, Chardin continued in much the same vein to the end of his still-life painting career. As he did so, he attended to relations among different kinds of singularity—single cups or glasses, unified masses of peaches or strawberries, stray bunches of grapes or stems of cherries, single grapes or peaches—not to mention different kinds of reflectivity, and different contrasts between the matte and the shiny, the transparent and the opaque, reflected patches of color and the colored items that they reflect.[28] Those are the still lifes that might have interested Morandi, who has often been linked to Chardin, and with good reason.[29] But Morandi's specific engagement with such precedents as Chardin's later still lifes is not the point of these excursuses; on the contrary, I am more concerned with the question of what, in such still-life precursors, he refused to avail himself of. And high on the list of what he was *not* interested in was Chardin's (and many other still-life painters') fairly constant thematization of the relay between gastronomy and painting—or, to put it another way, between digestible and indigestible matter.

Excursus 6: Edouard Manet

But one painter who was interested in that topic was the first father of French modernist painting, Edouard Manet. Between 1862, when he painted a plate of oysters, and 1880, when he painted a single lemon, his still lifes ran the gamut from shopping, as in fish brought home with its wrapping; to cooking, as in the fish stew that is being prepared in the largish *Still Life with Fish* (1864) in the Art Institute of Chicago (figure 33); and to the eating of the depicted meal, as in the oysters. In those still lifes, Manet placed great emphasis on the materiality of his paint surfaces, nowhere more so than in the *Still Life with Fish*, which suggests a fairly direct equivalence between the dirty, fatty stain of fish oil on the represented cloth and the lipid substance of pigment suspended in oil medium with which it is rendered.[30] Riffing on Chardin's copper pots and kitchen scenes, Manet transformed Chardin's meditations on the relay between cooking and painting into a more pro-

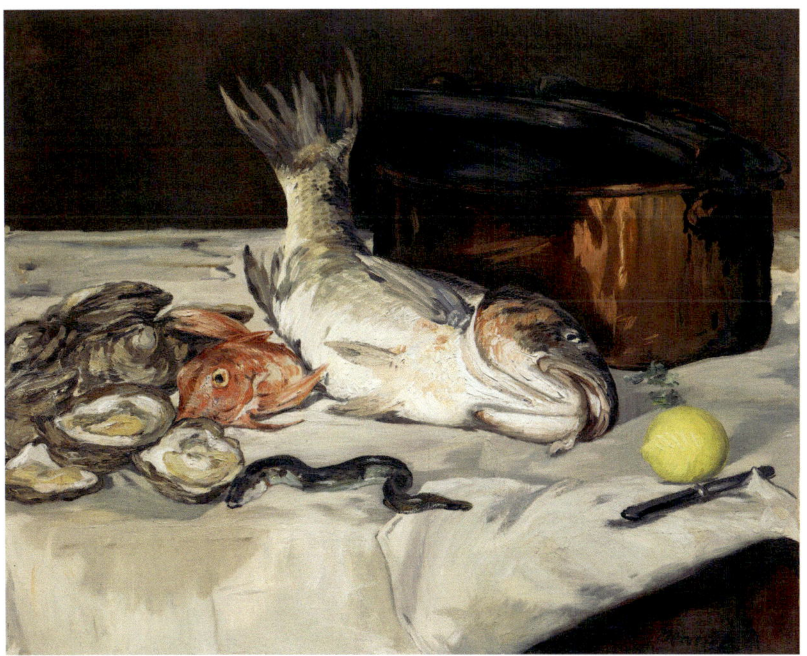

Figure 33. Edouard Manet, *Still Life with Fish*, 1864. Oil on canvas. 29 × 36 in. (73.5 × 92.4 cm). Art Institute of Chicago, Mr. and Mrs. Lewis Larned Coburn Memorial Collection. 1942.311.

nounced meditation on the metaphoric mouthfeel of painting itself, with much more playful self-reflexivity in his still-life subjects than anywhere else in his oeuvre. And then he shifted into the one-to-one equivalence between a slightly larger than life-size painting and a single item, a lemon, whose paintedness is made evident by Manet's rich, oily facture (figure 34). And this is no longer an illusionistic lemon for imaginative handling, cutting, squeezing, and seasoning something to eat, but a lemon just for looking at, closed off as it is inside its bright lemon peel, with no knife to cut into it. The invitation to bodily consumption is disallowed in favor of consumption by the eye alone.

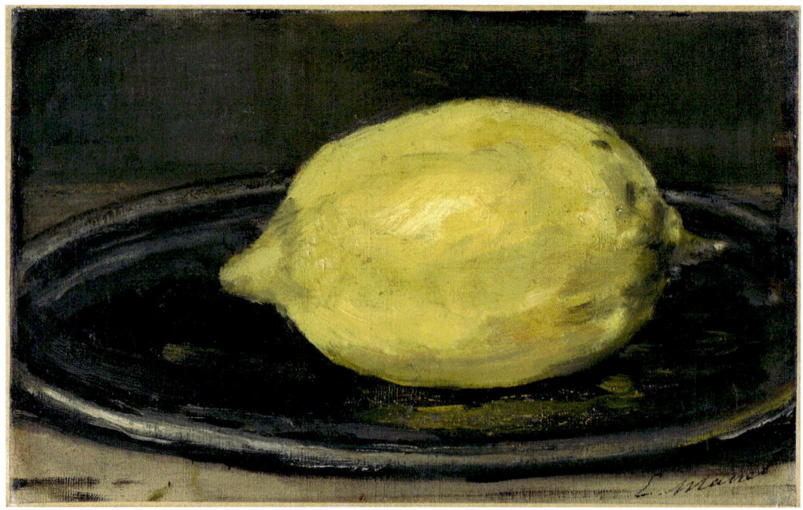

Figure 34. Edouard Manet, *The Lemon*, 1880. Oil on canvas. 5.5 × 8 in. (14 × 22 cm). Musée d'Orsay, Paris. Photo credit: © RMN-Grand Palais / Art Resource, NY.

Manet, who was known as a wit, loved his pictorial jokes, whether it was a matter of transforming one of Chardin's hanging dead rabbits—which he also riffed on in his own painting of a dead rabbit—into a hanging blossom cut from the garden, not to be eaten, of course, but to go into a vase for looking at; or chivalrously sending his friend Berthe Morisot a painted note, a painted fan, and a painted bunch of violets in lieu of real ones; or of mailing to another friend, Isabelle Lemonnier, a handwritten note with a watercolored Mirabelle plum decorating it, in which he rhymed on her name and pitted words against image; or of gifting a painting of a single asparagus to his patron Charles Ephrussi, who had commissioned a painting of a bundle of asparagus for 800 francs but then paid 1000 francs, and to whom Manet said when he sent the single asparagus—as if to make up the difference and point to the question of monetary value—"There is one missing from your bunch."[31] The last instance of Manet's still-life joking is to be found in the foreground of his famous *Bar at the Folies-Bergère*. Signing his name on the label of the Campari bottle on the left side of the painting, and the date, too, as if to say that 1882 was a very good year, Manet quipped about the commodity status of his own painting, while also refuting the abstraction of exchange value with the luscious thingness of his painting qua painting, all in the zone of still life.[32] And thus he upped the ante on the genre's tradition of material thought about itself, thereby putting still life front and center stage in modernism's auto-referential game.

Excursus 7: Henri Fantin-Latour

Throughout his still-life painting practice, Manet competed with his friend the still-life specialist Henri Fantin-Latour. Indeed, it was that painter who gave him the idea of dedicating a single painting to a single object, which Fantin-Latour first did in the early 1860s, most notably in his delicate little 1864 picture of a white teacup and saucer with a silver spoon, now in the Fitzwilliam Museum in Cambridge (figure 35). It, too, is approximately the life-size of the item(s) depicted. As if borrowing the darkness that surrounds such items from Cotán's, Zurbaran's, and Kalf's still lifes, and lifting the teacup and its saucer from his own more elaborate compositions—while also removing any decorative embellishment from around the inner and outer porcelain surfaces of the cup-and-plate duo—Fantin-Latour zeroes in on the object-to-painting/painting-to-object relationship that has been the theme of these excursuses.

Crafting the crafted china in paint—blacks and whites, grays, and hints of yellow-brown—Fantin-Latour plays in the interstices between porcelain and pigment, carving out the hollow of the cup with just a slight adjustment of his whites; rounding its volume with a sequence of subtly planar gray shifts; picking out the arc of its delicate handle by means of the little black space that is cupped within it; attaching that handle to the cup with a touch of whitest white; edging the rim of the saucer against the black that

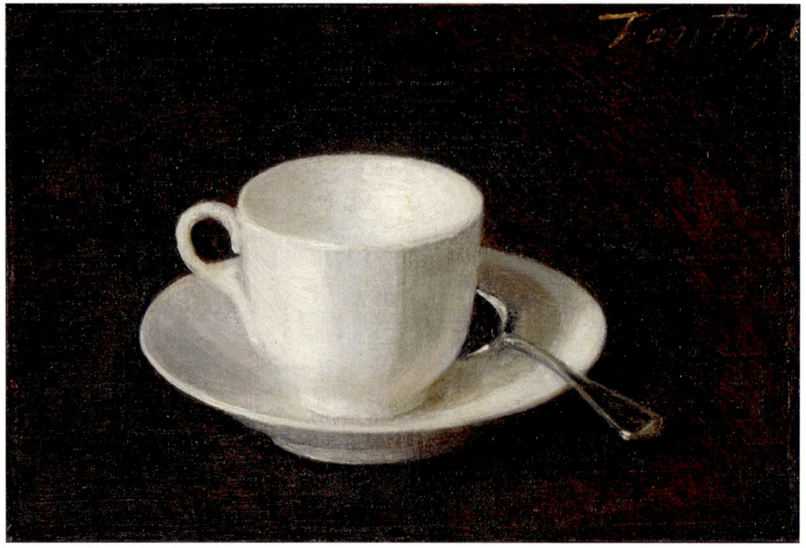

Figure 35. Henri Fantin-Latour, *White Cup and Saucer*, 1864. Oil on canvas. 7 × 11 in. (19.4 × 28.9 cm). Photograph © The Fitzwilliam Museum, University of Cambridge.

surrounds it with just a gleam of that brightest white; placing hints of the same brilliant white on the base of the cup as well as on the handle and bowl of the silver teaspoon; pooling some dishwater color in the saucer to create both the dip in its shape and the shadow that puddles within it like so much spilt tea. Out of the simplest and most fragile of cup-and-saucers a painting has been made, but equally, out of the simplest and most subtle of paintings has a cup-and-saucer been fabricated.

The *White Cup and Saucer* is a painting in which the spotlit singularity of its object(s) comes into question—is it one thing, or two or three that is/are depicted here?—along with the gentle disturbances to balance and symmetry that emerge from the slightly off-center placement of the cup on its saucer, and in turn of the cup-and-saucer within the rectangularly framed black field that it inhabits. These are things that have been noted by other viewers, for several writers have been drawn to pick out this little work from all others housed in the Fitzwilliam Museum and write about it evocatively: "Just that and little more. The picture is an act of strict isolation," wrote Tom Lubbock of the *Independent* in 2008, going on to remark, "These simple, normal things attract metaphors, become metaphoric. You can notice, for instance, that a cup-and-saucer is not a singular thing."[33] Most recently, Ali Smith chose "this tiny glowing and haunting painting, ostensibly a momentary nothing in life [but] . . . really an everything" from among all the more grandiloquent of the Fitzwilliam Museum's possessions for a pandemic-lockdown elegy: "No mythology? No gods? No flourish of art? No beautiful colourful intricate vase? No protective suit of armour the size of a giant? / No. / . . . The kind of picture . . . where light and dark create something so ordinary-looking and yet so blastingly uncanny that it's like a prophecy in itself, a reminder to everyone who sees it of the strangeness all through our lives, and of how fragile and tough and surreal, everything that's everyday to us can be."[34] That's as a good a summation as I can think of, of the attractions of still-life painting more generally.

And A.S. Byatt, author of the 1985 novel *Still Life*, also spoke about Fantin-Latour's teacup in 2008. She spoke of the "domestic trap" of "tea table chatter, the generations of potters from whom she was descended, the "'mystery' of craftmanship," learning about "clay and glazes and kilns and furnaces," and "the almost infinite complexity of all the processes and materials that go into the provision of a simple cup of tea," citing William Blake and W.H. Auden as she went on about the "doors of perception" and the "'lane to the land of the dead'" opened up by a crack in a teacup.[35] Thus Fantin-Latour's "beautifully crafted painting about a beautifully crafted cup, saucer and spoon" opens onto a large world of associations with the making and using of porcelain teacups. It is also a painting that makes me fast-forward to Edmund de Waal's fascination with porcelain (and his own serried arrays of pale-glazed, slightly wonky ceramic objects)—but does so in pictorial terms, which also make me think of the kinship between Morandi and de Waal.[36] And the whiteness of the cup-and-saucer? Confected out of the close connection between white paint and white glaze, it, too, makes me think ahead to Morandi's white-painted bottles—though I cannot suppose that Fantin-Latour would have been among Morandi's go-to artists of the French modernist canon.

Excursus 8: Paul Cézanne

But Paul Cézanne *was* one of those artists, though largely in the domain of landscape painting; the effect of his still lifes on Morandi is mostly felt secondhand, filtered through the later Cubist refraction of Cézanne's work.[37] Cézanne must nonetheless figure into these digressions on the history of material thought offered up by the genre of still life. For, as one of the many French still-life painters in the second half of the nineteenth century who sometimes took Chardin as their model—both Manet and Fantin-Latour were among them too—Cézanne can stand as a bridge between the eighteenth-century painter's ruminations on the materiality of paint, artifact, and food and the twentieth-century inheritance of the modernist insistence on the paintedness of painting. For that, I turn to one early still life from 1866, when Cézanne was still in the throes of his youthful Manet fixation, in the Musée Granet in Cézanne's hometown of Aix-en-Provence: *Sugar Bowl, Pears, and Blue Cup* (figure 36).[38] I do so in part because of its closeness to the Chardin model, with its attachment to everyday domestic objects that belonged in and to the painter's home, and in part because of its intimate size, which brings it both close to hand and close to the diminutive scale of Morandi's work.

Palette-knifed and heavily impastoed, Cézanne's *Sugar Bowl, Pears, and Blue Cup* replaces all of the reflective and refractive, transparent and translucent, texturally differentiated effects of the illusionist still life with an almost sculptural handling—here paint is more like potter's clay than paint-

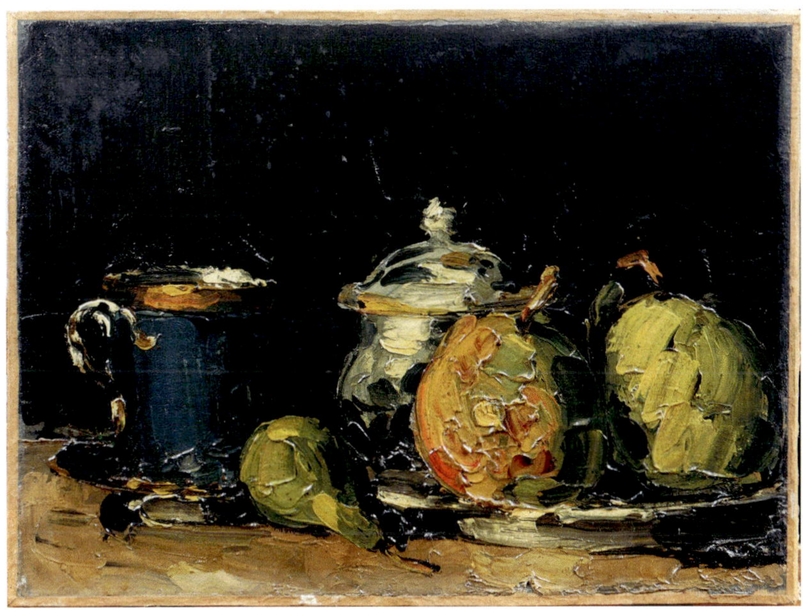

Figure 36. Paul Cézanne, *Sugar Bowl, Pears, and Blue Cup*, ca. 1866. Oil on canvas. 12 × 16 in. (30 × 41 cm). Musée Granet, Aix-en-Provence. Photo credit: © RMN-Grand Palais / Art Resource, NY.

er's medium—that drives home the fact that the painting is a made material thing, a very physical and in that sense a real rather than fictive object. Here one has the feeling not only of seeing each mark made with the loaded palette knife, but also of the single medium out of which all the assorted still-life items are made, whether they be blue and gilt coffee cup, or white figured sugar container with its lid sitting squarely atop itself, or three pears—one small loose one and two fat ones sitting atop a plate, whose rim is marked by several bold swipes—or brown wooden ledge or tabletop and black empty background space: all are self-evidently made of thick oil paint rather than ceramic, fruit flesh, wood, or air, joined together in a single, dense surface. This is distinctly indigestible matter, and as such, it turns the tables on still life's history of using its own materiality to evoke the materiality of other things, insisting instead—as Morandi would do in different terms—on its own gluey substance, its own handmade substantiality. No coffee is offered for drinking, no sugar for sweetening, no hint of the pears' outer skin or interior pith and juice—the toothsomeness of this coagulated little painting is all the toothsomeness of slathered oil paint—and also little optical appeal, for any gleam and glisten that attaches to it is that which adheres to the ridges and crests of the paint material as the light catches in it. What there is instead is the overt tactility of the painted thing, circling claustrophobically back on itself.

A short postscript on Cézanne: among his many later still lifes is one watercolor that features a lone object, *The Green Pitcher* of 1887 (figure 37). Also a small work keyed to the size of the item it portrays, it is painted in the lightly faceted manner that interested so many twentieth-century painters, including Morandi. Indeed, its anthropomorphism might have appealed to Morandi too: with its two handles approximating head and akimbo arm and the swelling sides of its corpulent body a belly and buttocks, it looks for all the world like a fat green Buddha. But it is the white highlight punctuating the hip turned toward us that catches the eye: made of the same blank paper that is visible elsewhere in the composition, it constitutes an inversion of all those white-painted highlights in the history of still-life painting on up through Morandi's own work. Like a hole in the green and gray-blue watercolor and graphite-made glaze of the portly little pot, it allows us to peer through its optical gleam, which it turns inside out, to the tactile heft of its real paper surface.[39]

Excursus 9: William and Ben Nicholson

My ninth and last excursus concerns an early twentieth-century British father-and-son pair—namely, William and Ben Nicholson. It is unlikely that Morandi would have known of William Nicholson's Edwardian still lifes,

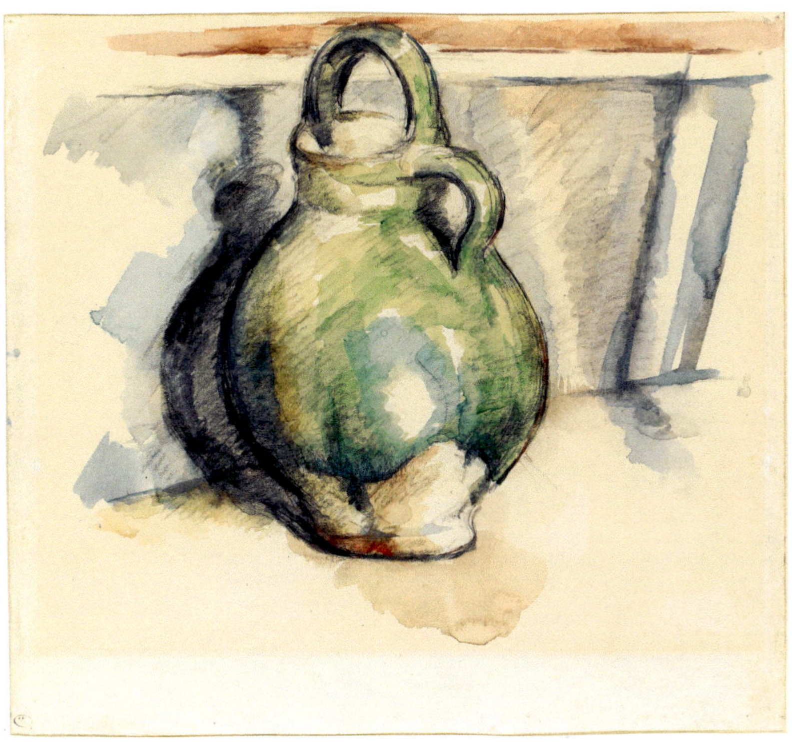

Figure 37. Paul Cézanne, *The Green Pitcher*, 1887. Watercolor. 8½ × 10 in. (22 × 24.7 cm). Musée d'Orsay, Paris. Photo credit: © RMN-Grand Palais / Art Resource, NY.

such as the lovely *Lustre Bowl with Green Peas* of 1911 (figure 38), though it is possible that he may have encountered Ben Nicholson's work in Italy, as, for example, in the Venice Biennale of 1954; certainly the younger Nicholson, who lived and traveled in Italy off and on, was an admirer of Morandi, remarking that the latter was "the person who continues my father's art. He is the link between his art and mine. I always paint my still lives with Morandi in mind."[40] If Ben Nicholson had begun in a William Nicholson mode, by the time of that remark his still-life canvases—like his father's,

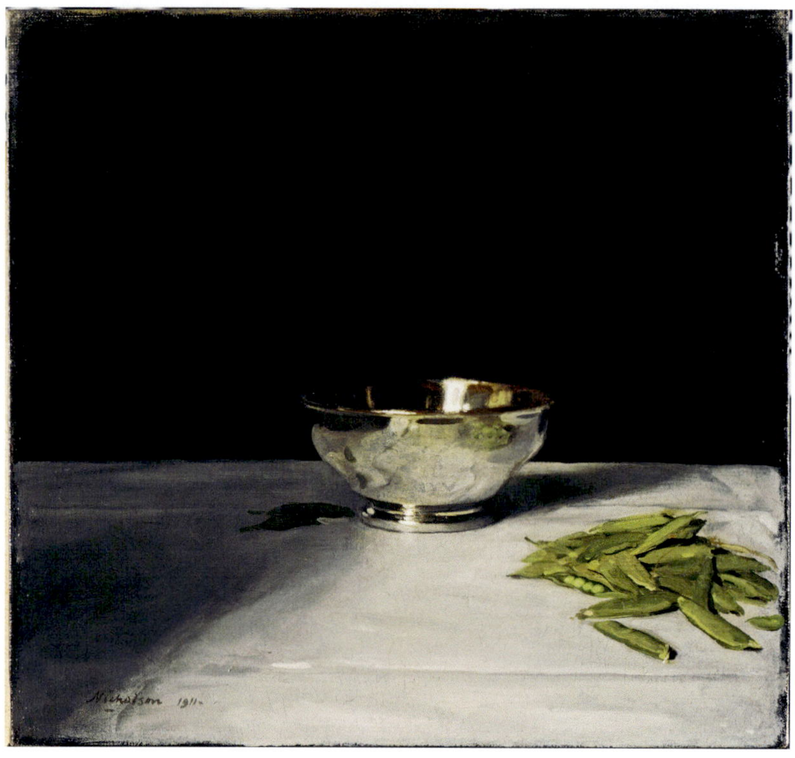

Figure 38. William Nicholson, *The Lustre Bowl with Green Peas*, 1911. Oil on canvas. 21 1/2 × 23 1/2 in. (55 × 60 cm). National Galleries of Scotland, Edinburgh. Bequest of Lady Murray of Henderland 1861.

most of his work belonged to that category—looked more like the scored, cubistic composition of the 1948 *Still Life, Crystal*, presently in the Milwaukee Museum of Art (figure 39), in which it is certainly possible to see Morandi as the middle term between Nicholson père and fils.

As a still-life painter, William Nicholson was a latter-day Chardinian: the *Lustre Bowl with Green Peas* takes up the play of reflection and reflected object (white cloth and green peas reflected in the side of the bowl) and sets

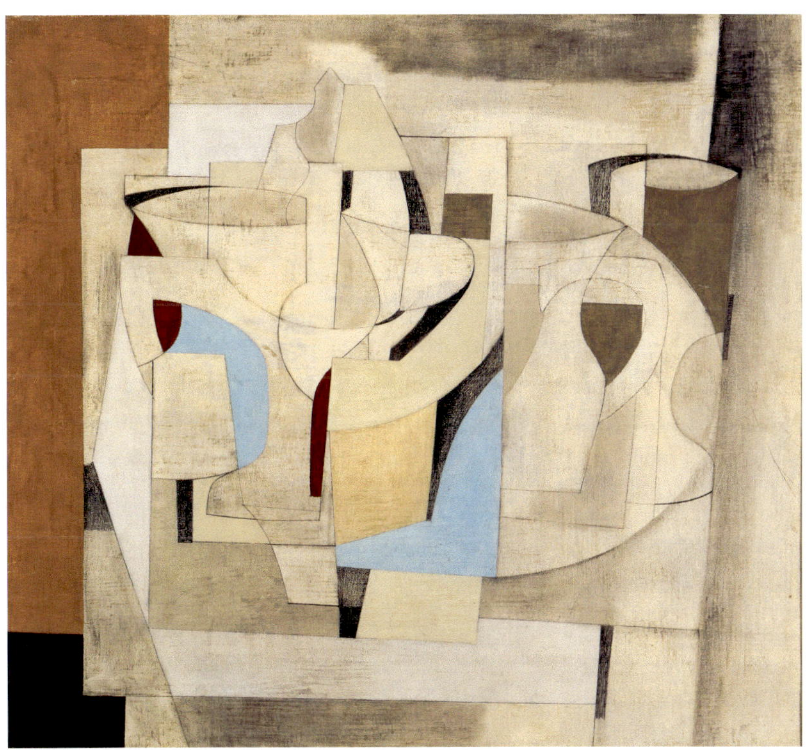

Figure 39. Ben Nicholson, *Still Life, Crystal*, 1948. Oil and pencil on canvas, 24 × 26 3/4 in. (61 × 68 cm). Milwaukee Art Museum, gift of Friends of Art, M1958.8. © Angela Verren Taunt. All rights reserved, DACS, London / ARS, NY 2025, © Artists Rights Society (ARS), New York / United Kingdom, DACS. Photographer credit: John R. Glembin. http://www.mam.org.

it side by side with an intimation of kitchen or dining use (the shelling of peas), and within the aura of domestic space, as hinted at both in the squared creases of the tablecloth and in the streak of windowlight cradled in the curved interior of the silver vessel. And the white highlight gleams on the lusterware are all of a piece with the European history of still-life painting, as is the hushed dark background, which seems to sacralize the shadow-enshrouded, shadow-casting bowl.

Gone is all of that in the younger Nicholson's *Still Life, Crystal*, which is nonetheless just a little larger than the dimensions of the *Still Life with Lustre Bowl*. In its place? The shuttling of dark background space to fill in the lower left corner, and to color in the interstices between not things but pencil-delineated shapes and areas of intricate, pencil-indicated overlay. The laying down of brown, as if derived from the referencing of wooden tabletop, all along the far left sector of the painting, abutting the (wooden) framed edge of the canvas. Next to that, a large expanse of modulated, penciled, off-white tone suggesting an object-laden table. Areas of shading, some helping to carve out the interior hollows of pitcher and goblet forms, some detached from that function, some turning flat, solid gray as if to attach themselves first to the surfaces of almost-represented things and then to the real plane of the actual canvas. Pops of color like the two zones of sky blue that hover among slivers of maroon and tan and gray and white, like displaced puzzle pieces moving ambiguously between surface and background hue. And everywhere, self-contradictory evocations of transparency and see-through overlap, everywhere asserting, everywhere refuting themselves in the opaque singleness of the canvas, as if to simultaneously illustrate and undermine the "crystal" of the painting's subtitle. Many objects to the one eponymous thing of the *Still Life with Lustre Bowl*, but none of them are there except as pencil-and-paint ghosts of the real pitchers and goblets that sat in Ben Nicholson's studio and to which he was as attached as Morandi was to the denizens of his three tabletops.

Or perhaps it is better to declare, as the painting itself seems to do, that those pencil-and-paint ghosts are the traces of the artist's repeated *seeing* of his pitchers and goblets next to and through and in relation to each other. For those ghosts are also dematerializations of the objects, and the relationships among them, that are mapped and diagrammed within the materialized plane of the canvas. As such, they resemble Morandi's penciled "ground plan"—just as Nicholson's abstract white reliefs look like variations on that same "ground plan," but in pared down, built up, sculpted form—reducing the framed object groupings found in the history of still life to the play of the round and the rectangular, curve and angle, circle, square and quadrilateral, and to the intersection of plan and elevation, ground plane and cross section.[41] Which is to say that now, rather than using one materiality—that of oil paint—to evoke and play on a set of other materialities, the younger Nicholson has thinned out the diverse materialities of the object world within the thickened materiality of the canvas, swapping out the former for the latter. I do not believe that this was ever still life's telos, but this is one place where the genre's thematized play of mind and matter happened to land, three and half centuries after it took flight.

MORANDI'S THIRD AREA

Which brings me back, finally, to Morandi's little still life, and the difference between his form of still-life materialism and that of twentieth-century abstraction, which is where I want to close. On the one hand, there is the fact that Morandi avoided almost all of the illusionisms that I have discussed as part of the still-life tradition's thought about materiality. On the other hand, there is the fact that he insisted on the tangible reality of both the objects represented and the object doing the representing, the painting itself. As I have tried to show, what still life does more than any other genre of representational painting is to trade on the self-reflexive involvement of its own materiality as painting in the materialities of the world. We have seen this throughout the other still-life paintings I have addressed, but Morandi puts it forcefully and very stringently, drawing a very tight connection between paint and object matter. Thus, rather than withdrawing from representation into abstraction, Morandi focused a contracted and exacting light on the materialism—and also the existentialism—of the representational act.

Indeed, we might say that Morandi did in paint, and with his gessoed and painted objects, what his British contemporary Donald Woods

Winnicott did for the theory of object relations in mid-twentieth-century psychoanalysis. Winnicott understood playing with objects as the child's way of bridging the divide between the inner world of the imagination and the outer world of the real: a way of making that inner world *real* in what Winnicott called a "third" or "intermediate area," also a "potential space"—a zone mediating between subjective experience and objective reality that holds inner and outer worlds in paradoxical suspension. (Here I should note that Winnicott understood the inner world of the human subject not as a set of emotional states that needed to be released, but rather as a psychic region—a kind of fantasy space—that required "me-extensions" to externalize itself in the physical world of the "not-me"; the "third area" was thus a relational space of subject-object intersections rather than of projection or self-expression.) In turn, Winnicott described all adult creativity and culture as continuations and expansions of that "third area" in which the child's imaginative play with objects takes place, beginning to write that theory up in the 1950s and then publishing it as a book of collected essays, titled *Playing and Reality*, in 1971, seven years after Morandi's death.[42] What I'd like to propose here is that that, too, is exactly what Morandi did with still lifes such as the 1956 painting with which I began: he used his painted objects to forge a connection with external reality. He used the materiality of paint to externalize his inner life and make it real by connecting it up with the reality of the world outside himself. And in so doing, he not only conjoined abstraction and realism, he also showed why painting matters, and what Cézanne had meant when he said, as he did, that "the painter thinks in painting."[43]

But let us first see how Morandi got there. While still a student—and concurrently a drawing master—at the Accademia di Belle Arti in Bologna, he began painting still lifes, in a context that neither valued the lowest of the genres nor rewarded modernist experimentation. Following a short involvement in the Futurist movement, and then a stint in the Italian Army in 1915, which ended abruptly in a breakdown, Morandi settled into a post as a local inspector of drawing pedagogy, which would last until 1930, when he became professor of etching at the same Accademia di Belle Arti where he had been both student and drawing master. At the same time, he hunkered down into the painting of still life and spent thirty to forty years making it his own. Did the rupture of his war experience play into that hunkering down?[44] Of course it is hard to say for sure, and I have no intention of treating Morandi as a trauma victim, or his still-life practice as a biographically determined form of art-as-therapy. It does, however, seem plausible to me—and consistent with Winnicott's particular take on object relations theory—that Morandi's tabletop world functioned as a specific kind of experimental space over which he could exert some control, and in which he could explore the ratio of instability to stability in a world doubly of his own making, in a detached and specifically pictorial way. In that sense, then, I do suspect that still life became a kind of pictorial safe space for the Bolognese painter, who rather insistently mythologized his retreat from the fray of public life and the larger art world beyond Bologna.[45] A safe space that was also a "third area" of serious play, in which he could move his objects around like so many chess pieces, paint them and repaint them, and thereby both externalize and stabilize what was unstable within and without himself.

Morandi's earliest still lifes (from 1914, just before he joined the army) have the look of derivative "analytical Cubism," clearly emulating Braque's early monochrome still lifes from the period around 1909. But immediately after his return from military service, Morandi began to put aside all obvious gestures to Cubism, except for the monochromatic register that had been one of its signature features. In 1916 we see him casting around. First he tried for a flattened and solidified Picassoid monumentality, with one thing placed squarely next to another in the front plane, as in the vertical still life in New York's Museum of Modern Art (figure 40), with its black bottle, gray tin pitcher, tan bottle, and gray cafetière all placed on a table that seems to

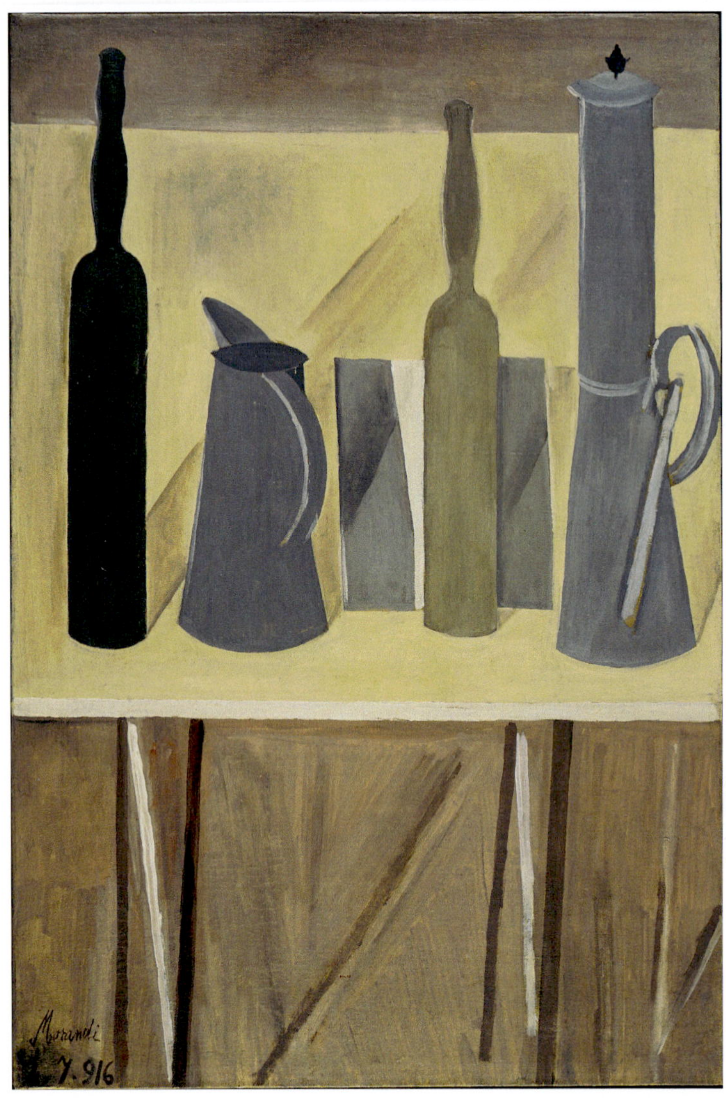

Figure 40. Giorgio Morandi, *Still Life*, 1916. Oil on canvas. 32½× 22⅝ in. (82.5 × 57.5 cm). Museum of Modern Art, NY, Acquired through the Lillie P. Bliss Bequest (by exchange). © 2024 Artists Rights Society (ARS), New York / SIAE, Rome.

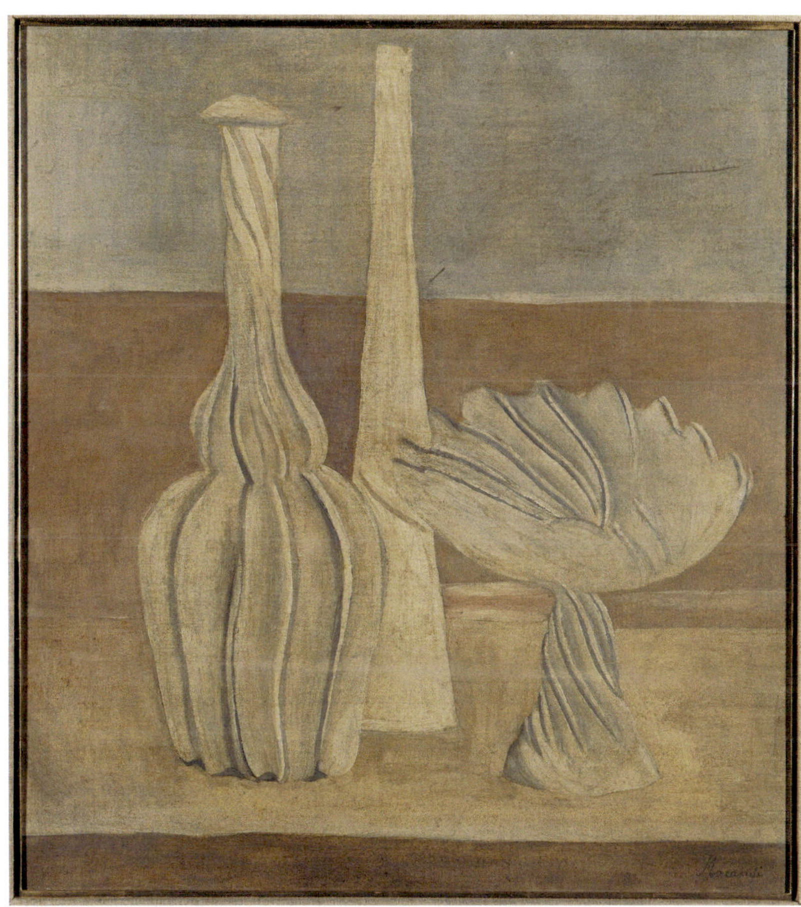

Figure 41. Giorgio Morandi, *Natura Morta*, 1916. Oil on canvas. 23 × 22 in. (60 × 54 cm). Gianni Mattioli Collection, MATTIOLI/PEGGY GUGGENHEIM. © ARS, NY. Photo credit: Scala / Art Resource, NY.

double as an easel. Next he aimed for something more organic and intimate, which broke free of Cubist precedent, and began to reverse still life's game of equivalent materialities, by means of literally digging into and building up his increasingly pallid paint surfaces, scoring them to flute his bottle and fruit dish, as if seeking to craft his still-life items within painting's own material terms (figure 41).

Let me linger for a moment in the period around 1920, for those years were marked by more diversity of approach than would be the case later on. In 1919 Morandi shuttled between simplified, linear variations on Cézannian still-life motifs, with all textural and coloristic variation removed, and a short foray into the domain of Scuola Metafisica painting, which served to further pare down all the material evocations of the genre into a taut monochromatic linearity that drained the represented object world of all substance and specificity, as in a *natura morta* in Milan's Pinacoteca di Brera (figure 42).[46] There a sliced half of a mannequin head lies on its side in the midst of one white bottle and two nameless cylindrical objects, also laid on their sides—one thin and mustard colored, the other white and thicker in circumference—and one upright white fruit dish, all casting minimal shadows on a flattened, nondescript ground whose three horizontal yellow-taupe strips are meant to represent the front plane of a ledge, the horizontal surface on which the objects rest, and the background plane, respectively. But those three planes are abstracted into one, while the laid-on-their-sides objects, removed of all surface detail and barely distinguished from their surrounds, look like so many Uccello-esque orthogonals in a perspectival diagram, as if foreshadowing Morandi's later "ground plan." Meanwhile the three whitened objects predict his gessoed bottles: it was as if the flirtation with "metaphysical" painting, short-lived as it was, gave Morandi the means to clean house and set the blank-slate stage for his later gaming in still life's "third area." It was also the closest he came to the dematerialization of the object world that describes abstractionist work such as Ben Nicholson's.

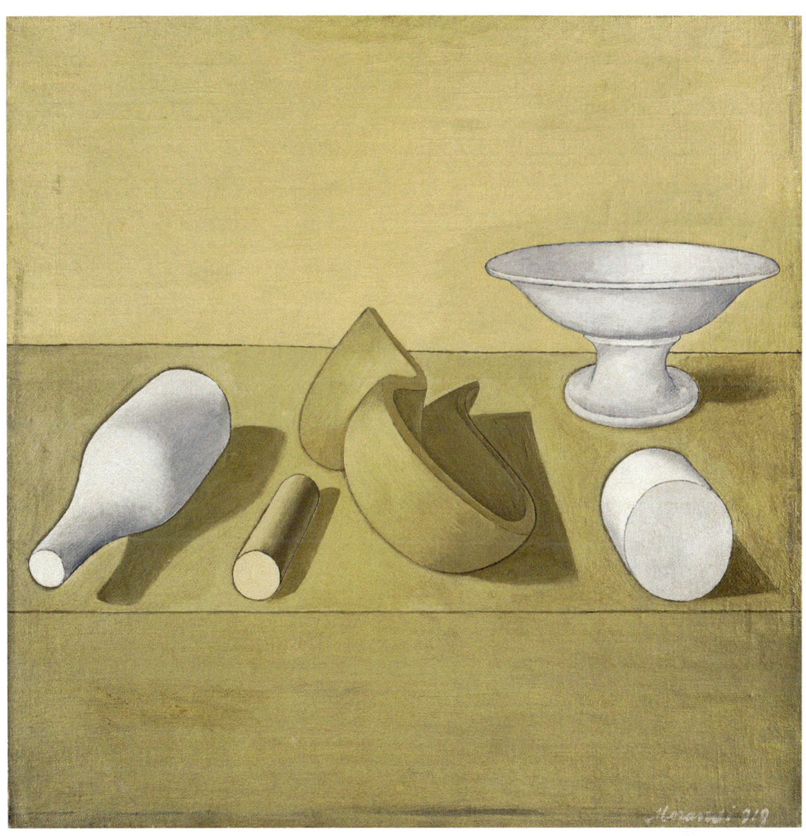

Figure 42. Giorgio Morandi, *Natura Morta*, 1919. Oil on canvas. 23.4 × 23.6 in. (68.5 × 72 cm). Pinacoteca di Brera, Milan. ©Pinacoteca di Brera, Milano © 2025 Artists Rights Society (ARS), New York / SIAE, Rome.

For in 1920 Morandi returned to the depiction of materialized objects, as in the blond-toned Düsseldorf still life in the Cézannian mode (figure 43), replete with its bread rolls and white napkin on a tabletop, but this time with three glinting glass objects—including the unusual little gilt-decorated blue vase on the right—a projecting knife, equally unusual for Morandi, and an overturned white bowl. The projecting knife stands as a signifier of the still-life tradition—and all of the illusionist tricks associated with it—that Morandi would simultaneously embrace and reject, while the surface decoration on the blue vase and the highlights on transparent glass and white ceramic index the triple bind in which he found himself, caught as he was between still life's resources for evoking the textured materiality of the object world and his own inclination toward vacating those very resources, while nonetheless asserting the shared materiality of painting and painted thing. That was more or less a one-off, however, as was another experiment from 1920, the chiaroscural, Rembrandt-brown still life in the Guggenheim Museum in Bilbao that sets four objects similarly side by side (figure 44). But now the surrounds of those four objects are reduced to two strips, marked by the slightest of tonal differentiation, and the frontal side-by-sideness of the objects is stark and unrelieved by any gesture to overlap or fore-and-aft placement. And as for the four objects—a brown ball, an upright brown cylinder, a whitened bottle, and the same overturned white bowl as before—in addition to their reduction of the illusionist resources of oil painting to the volumetric effects of modeling and shading, they state the case, as plain as can be, for a constricted materiality and a short-circuiting of the opposition between the abstract and the representational.

Already by the mid-1920s, Morandi had begun to settle into his signature still-life preoccupations: the varied repetition, in a severely restrained palette, of a narrow, undescribed table space with mostly matte objects lined up in the front zone, shallowly overlapping one another so that the intervals between objects begin to count, registering ambiguously as tense and pressured. For some forty years, that would be the name of the game, punctuated here and there by exceptions that prove the rule. For example, several times in the mid- to late 1920s, Morandi would step back from the uppermost of his three tables in order to take in its curved front edge and lip along with a more global view of the crowd of objects on its surface, as in the almost

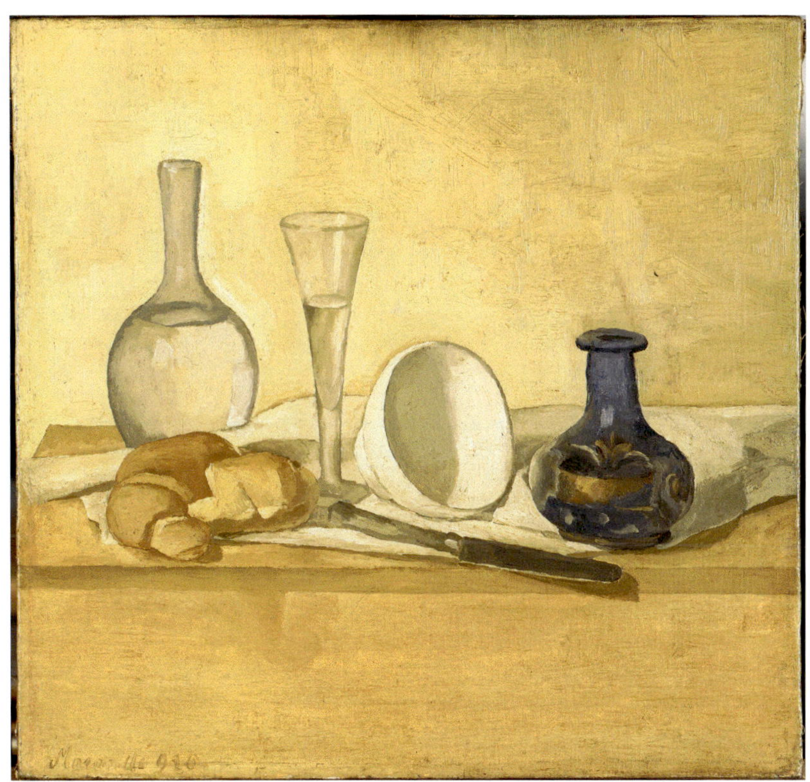

Figure 43. Giorgio Morandi, *Still Life*, 1920. Oil on canvas. 19 1/2 × 20 1/2 in. (49.5 × 52 cm). Düsseldorf Kunstsammlung, Nordrhein-Westfalen. bpk Bildagentur / Art Resource, NY. © ARS, NY.

square still life of 1929, also in the Pinacoteca di Brera (figure 45). There a pale pink teapot and a blue kerosene-lamp base stand out from the brown to taupe gloom embracing the closely jammed crowd of six to seven vertical objects and two horizontal plates. Meanwhile, one strong highlight is striped down the side of one of the bottles in the center—echoed by two more muted gleams to the right of it—so as to mark and interrupt the lusterlessness of the whole, and stand in contrast and comparison to the stark whiteness of the

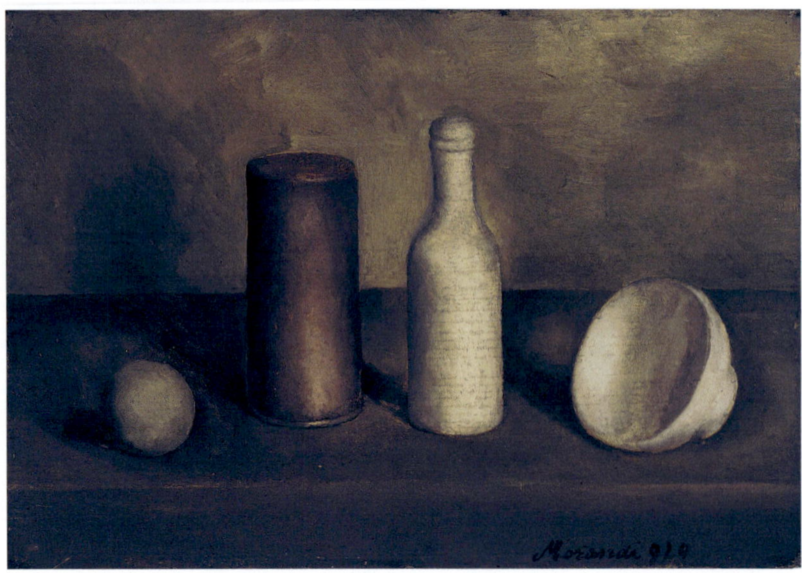

Figure 44. Giorgio Morandi, *Natura Morta*, 1920. Oil on canvas. 12 × 17½ in. (30.5 × 44.5 cm). Museo Morandi.

two rightmost bottles, one more determinedly matte than the other: in this painting, it is as evident as can be that it is the same thick white paint that makes the different kinds of bright effect, whether it be optical glisten or tactile pigmentation.

The 1930s saw a thickening of Morandi's palette, such that background pushed forward to compete with foreground objects, "negative" with "positive" space, while those objects contracted and expanded in number, variety, and complexity of grouping. That decade also saw the flowering of Morandi's rich etching practice, including experiments in rendering gleam by the absence of ink within densely hatched fields of objects-and-ground—sometimes even rendering the objects themselves as white absences within those webs of hatching.[47] Again there are moments of punctuation by bright

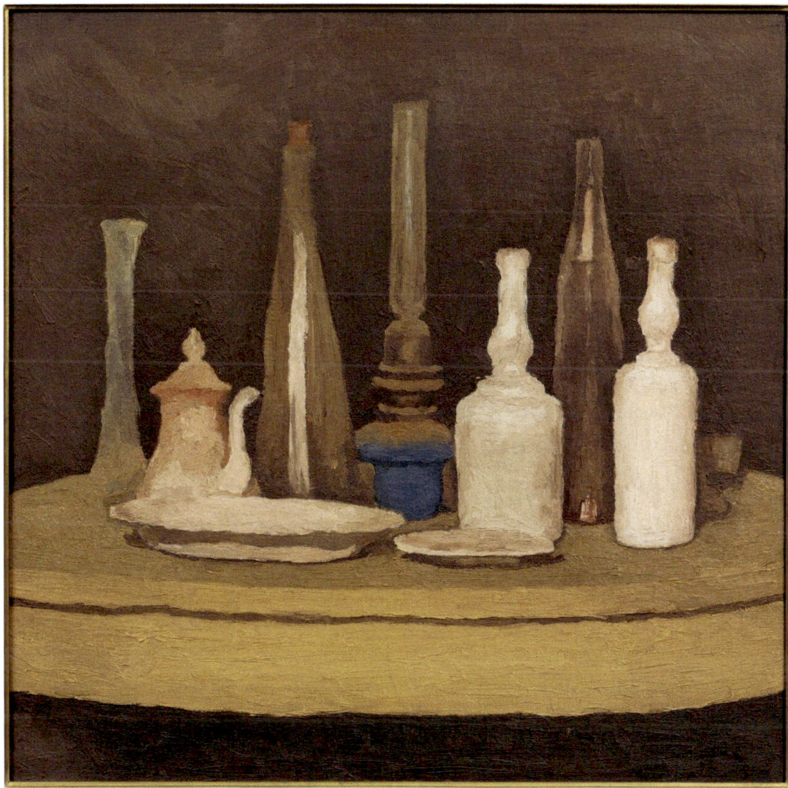

Figure 45. Giorgio Morandi, *Natura Morta*, 1929. Oil on canvas. 21 5/8 × 22 3/4 in. (67 × 89 cm). Pinacoteca di Brera, Milan. © Pinacoteca di Brera, Milano © 2025 Artists Rights Society (ARS), New York / SIAE, Rome.

color and strongly marked highlight—there are examples of this in the late 1930s. But sometimes—particularly in the early 1940s—such exceptions would be countered by smaller and larger arrays of all-white objects too. Move and countermove: that was Morandi's chessboard.

Around the turn of the 1940s into the '50s, Morandi made one last set of countermoves, exploring what it looked like when he expanded the space around his objects, either placing them on the sharp brink of nothingness at the back edge of one of his tables, or viewing them from overhead so as to look onto and into the tops of them while sometimes including glimpses of dramatic shadow and orthogonal flight into space. These were countermoves that seemed expressly designed to think materially about the opposition between matter, solid or otherwise, and the absence of matter. If the large majority of Morandi's still lifes, all the way from the 1920s to the '60s, were as explicit as it was possible to be about the equation between painting's material ground—its gessoed support—and the painted materiality of the objects it depicts, generalizing that materiality to the bare fact of solid substance, these other countermoves plotted their juxtapositions between crowded objects and expanded spaces in order to dramatize the confrontation between thing and no-thing.

But countermoves these were: different ways of marking the artist's more usual maneuvers. From the 1950s into the '60s, Morandi most often returned to the eye-level, frontal array of a limited number of objects against a nondescript two-toned ground evidently meant to stand for the meeting of the vertical plane of background wall and the horizontal plane of table surface. Sometimes a set of dark, undescribed objects are set behind more specified objects at more or less exactly the height of their tops, so as to both mediate and question the distinction between things and their surrounds. (And sometimes, one of the front row of objects will be turned slightly askew, as if to problematize the frontality of the rest, and test the limits of the generalization of objects that seems to go with it.) At other times, objects would be jammed so close to each other that the contour of one seems to provide, redefine, and cut into the contour of another. Less countermoves, these were variations on the same chess gambits that Morandi had been making since at least the 1930s. Had the game progressed? Had he moved forward? Had his work developed, his career advanced? Well, no, less that than expanded and contracted, settled and unsettled, and circled back

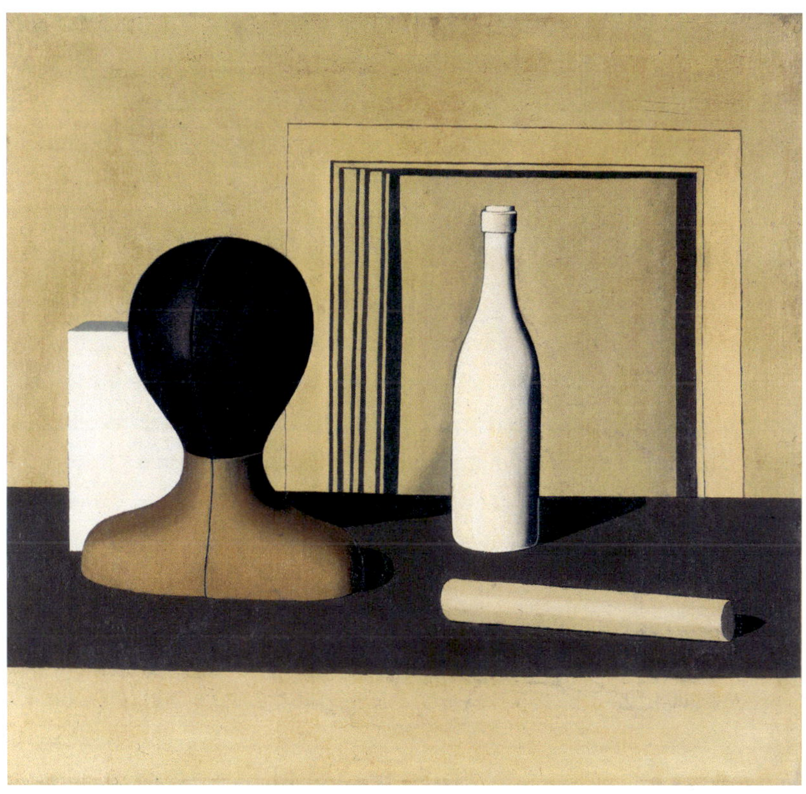

Figure 46. Giorgio Morandi, *Natura Morta*, 1918. Oil on canvas. 27 × 28 3/8 in. (68.5 × 72 cm). Pinacoteca di Brera, Milan.

around again and again, with small variations in arrangement, palette, format, and facture.

And so, let me end by returning to the beginning, and to a 1918 still life of the Scuola Metafisica period, again in the Pinacoteca di Brera in Milan (figure 46). For this is a still-life composition that might serve as an allegory of Morandi's "third area": consisting of an upright white bottle set against a rectangular molding that might be either a picture- or a doorframe, a taupe cylinder lying on its side, a blank, dark dummy head, and a glimpse of a vertical white box denuded of all detail, it also seems to depict a face-off between "me" and "not-me"—between subject and object, in short. That is, the head of the lay figure functions as a kind of *rückenfigur* stand-in for the seeing self, while the white bottle—predicting all those white-gessoed bottles and painted vessels to come—looks to be a kind of ur-object, the frame on the other side of it doubling as the framed pictorial space of painting and as an opening onto an unseen, offstage space. Meanwhile the linear manner of the whole, together with the blanking out of the dark mannequin head and the white bottle, renders the opposition between them a diagrammatic one. But also a contradictory one, for they are drawn together in kinship as well, in a "third area" between this and the other side of the canvas, between the internal zone of the viewer and manipulator of objects and the externality of the object world, which is at once found and made.[48] Not to mention between thought and matter, the abstract and the representational, illusory and real materiality.

In the mid-1920s, Morandi portrayed himself twice, holding a palette and facing the viewer, in a riff on a self-portrait by Manet. But it was in the 1918 "metaphysical" still life that he really portrayed himself—for there he represented himself not as a biographical individual, but rather in terms of the pictorial preoccupations that would haunt his still-life practice for decades to come. By the time of the 1956 Yale still life, those preoccupations had been revisited and revised repeatedly, but the paradox that was essential to Morandi's "third area" of serious play continued to be held in suspension: the object world that he found at home and in flea markets, that he gessoed and painted and then moved around on his tables, and that he then painted into his canvases—so that they became his material creations twice and thrice over—was also the space in which he concretized himself, externalizing his internal world in the material terms of paint, painting, and still-life picture making.

NOTES

PREFACE

1. I am indebted in particular to Marni Kessler, for her invitation to me to join her in designing the Franklin Murphy Seminar in the fall of 2020, which was titled, just as this book is, "The Matter of Still Life." That collaboration was both a real pleasure and an opportunity to learn from someone thoroughly immersed in the questions raised by the genre of still life, as witnessed in her beautifully observed and nuanced book, *Discomfort Food: The Culinary Imagination in Late Nineteenth-Century French Art* (University of Minnesota Press, 2021).

2. That early paper was written for a seminar on Dutch seventeenth-century painting taught by Svetlana Alpers at the University of California, Berkeley, which I took in the mid-1970s. My engagement in the topic of description is also much indebted to Alpers's groundbreaking book *The Art of Describing: Dutch Art in the Seventeenth Century* (University of Chicago Press, 1983). Even though the subject of that book is not descriptive writing per se, but rather a descriptive—as opposed to narrative—form of visual art, nonetheless its lessons, and its close attention to the lower genres, in which the Dutch excelled in the seventeenth century, have deeply informed my own thinking about such art.

3. See my *Still Lives* (Blurb Inc., 2012), which went through several iterations, finally including the beginnings of the essay on Morandi found in this book. As

for my engagement with the work of Diderot and Chardin, that first arose out of a graduate reading course on Diderot and the arts that I taught at Yale in the fall of 2017.

4. For an important milestone in the historiography of still life, see Norman Bryson, *Looking at the Overlooked: Four Essays on Still Life Painting* (Reaktion Books, 1990): while I do not agree with all of its arguments, that book established a kind of canon and set the terms for thinking through the abjectness of still life. (Prior to Bryson's book, the main overview of the European history of still-life painting had been Charles Sterling, *Still-Life Painting from Antiquity to the Present* [Harper & Row, 1981].)

5. For an early consideration of the colonial underpinnings of still life, see Julie Berger Hochstrasser, *Still Life and Trade in the Dutch Golden Age* (Yale University Press, 2007).

6. On the ekphrastic tradition, see Murray Krieger, *Ekphrasis: The Illusion of the Natural Sign* (Johns Hopkins University Press, 1992); James A. W. Heffernan, *Museum of Words: The Poetics of Ekphrasis from Homer to Ashbery* (University of Chicago Press, 1993); and John Hollander, ed., *The Gazer's Spirit: Poems Speaking to Silent Works of Art* (University of Chicago Press, 1995). On the incommensurability of word and image, see Michel Foucault, *The Order of Things: An Archaeology of the Human Sciences* (Random House Vintage Books, 1973), 9: ". . . the relation of language to painting is an infinite relation. . . . Neither can be reduced to the other's terms: it is in vain that we say what we see; what we see never resides in what we say . . ."

7. On the "material turn," see Jennifer L. Roberts, "Things: Material Turn, Transnational Turn," *American Art* 31, no. 2 (Summer 2019): 64–69; and Petra Lange-Berndt, ed., *Materiality* (Whitechapel Gallery, 2015).

8. For the classic articulation of "thing theory," see Bill Brown, ed., *Things* (University of Chicago Press, 2004), in particular his "Thing Theory" (first published in *Critical Inquiry* 28, no. 1 [Autumn 2001]: 1–22), which serves as the introduction to the book. See also Jane Bennett, *Vibrant Matter: A Political Ecology of Things* (Duke University Press, 2010).

9. On the question of "material thought," see my own *Cézanne's Gravity* (Yale University Press, 2018), which focuses on Cézanne's still lifes, as did my earlier *Cézanne in the Studio: Still Life in Watercolors* (J. Paul Getty Museum, 2004). For an anthropologist's view of the question, see Tim Ingold's thoughtful take on

"thinking through making," in *Making: Anthropology, Archaeology, Art and Architecture* (Routledge, 2013).

10. See Edmund de Waal, "Witness," in *Giorgio Morandi: Time Suspended*, ed. Marilena Pasquali (Skira, 2024), 45–53, 45.

1. CHARDIN, DIDEROT, AND THE MUTENESS OF MADE THINGS

1. Tom Lubbock, "Chardin, Jean-Baptiste Siméon: Glass of Water and Coffee Pot (1760)," *The Independent*, February 17, 2006, https://www.independent.co.uk/arts-entertainment/art/great-works/chardin-jeanbaptiste-simeon-glass-of-water-and-coffee-pot-1760-798010.html. For the full poem, see Tom Kuhn and David Constantine, eds., "Uncollected Poems 1931–33," *The Collected Poems of Bertolt Brecht* (Liveright Publishing [W.W. Norton], 2018), 449.

2. For the entry on "Encyclopédie," see Denis Diderot, *ARTFL Encyclopédie*, vol. 5, 635–49. For all of the *Encyclopedia* entries mentioned in this essay, I have consulted the University of Chicago's online ARTFL Encyclopédie Project: *Encyclopédie, ou dictionnaire raisonné des sciences, des arts et des métiers, etc.*, ed. Denis Diderot and Jean le Rond d'Alembert, University of Chicago: ARTFL Encyclopédie Project (Spring 2021 edition), ed. Robert Morrissey and Glenn Roe, http://encyclopedie.uchicago.edu/. (See also the Encyclopedia of Diderot & d'Alembert Collaborative Translation Project, University of Michigan, https://quod.lib.umich.edu/d/did/.) On Diderot's articles for the *Encyclopedia*, see Myrtille Méricam-Bourdet and Catherine Volpilhac, eds., *Diderot: Articles de l'Encyclopédie* (Gallimard, 2015). For the *Encyclopedia* plates, see John Lough, *Inventory of Diderot's Encyclopédie: Plates* (Liverpool University Press with the Voltaire Foundation, 1984); and Jacques Payen and Roger Lewinter, eds., *Diderot Encyclopedia: The Complete Illustrations 1762–1777*, 4 vols. and index (Harry N. Abrams, 1978). See also Paola Bertucci, *Artisanal Enlightenment: Science and the Mechanical Arts in Old Regime France* (Yale University Press, 2017); Daniel Brewer and Julie Candler Hayes, eds., *Using the* Encyclopédie*: Ways of Knowing, Ways of Reading* (Voltaire Foundation, 2002); Jacques Proust, *Diderot et l'Encyclopédie* (Armand Colin, 1967); and John Morley, *Diderot and the Encyclopaedists* (Chapman and Hall, 1884). See as well Simon Garfield, *All the Knowledge in the World: The Extraordinary History of the Encyclopedia* (Harper Collins, 2022).

3. In his *Essai sur la peinture*, published in tandem with the *Salon de 1765*, Diderot made his orientation toward the highest of the genres clear, writing "Ah! Si un sacrifice, une bataille, un triomphe, une scene publique pouvait être rendue avec la même verité dans tous ses details, qu'une scene domestique de Greuze ou de Chardin! / C'est sous ce point de vue surtout que le travail du peintre d'histoire est infiniment plus difficile que celui du peintre de genre" (Denis Diderot, *Essai sur la peinture*, chap. 5, "Paragraphe sur la Composition, où j'espère que j'en parlerai," in *Oeuvres de Diderot: Salons*, vol. 1, 478–79 [J. L. J. Brière, 1821]). Later, in the *Salon de 1769*, he complained that Chardin's facture did not serve his human figures as well as his still-life objects, finding the figure of the servant in the second version of *Une Femme qui revient du marché* (since destroyed) too colossal in her proportions and too mannered in her attitude: the sort of criticism that he never leveled at any of Chardin's still lifes (*Salon de 1769*, in Else Marie Bukdahl, Michel Delon, Didier Kahn, and Annette Lorenceau, eds., *Diderot: Salons IV: Héros et martyrs: Salons de 1769, 1771, 1775, 1781* [Hermann, 1995], 45). See also Shane Agin, "The Development of Diderot's Salons and the Shifting Boundary of Representational Language," in *Diderot Studies* 30 (2007): 11–29; and Michel Delon, "Les Essais sur la peinture ou la place de la théorie," in *Diderot Studies* 30 (2007): 31–51; Philippe Déan, *Diderot devant l'image* (Harmattan, 2000); Jean Starobinski, *Diderot dans l'espace des peintres* (Réunion des Musées Nationaux, 1992); Marc Eli Blanchard, "Writing the Museum: Diderot's Bodies in the *Salons*," in *Diderot: Digression and Dispersion, A Bicentennial Tribute*, ed. Jack Undank and Herbert Josephs (French Forum, Publishers, 1984), 21–36; and Else Marie Bukdahl, *Diderot critique d'art*, 2 vols. (Rosenkilde et Bagger, 1980).

4. For his three-page treatment of Van Loo's portrait of himself, see Denis Diderot, *Salon de 1767*, in *Oeuvres de Denis Diderot: Salons, Tome II* (J. L. J. Brière, 1821), 32–36: from a description of his appearance in the portrait, "sans perruque" and with "l'air du vieille coquette," Diderot moves to an explanation of his air of distraction (an interruption by "madame Van-Loo"), thence into a disquisition on the mobility and changeability of his own face, his preference for how he would like to be seen, and a comparison with other portraits of himself. (For the English translation, see John Goodman, trans., *Diderot on Art*, vol. 2, *The Salon of 1767* [Yale University Press, 1995], 19–21.) See also Daniel Brewer, "Portraying Diderot," in Undank and Josephs, *Diderot: Digression and Dispersion*, 44–59.

5. For the famous, lengthy treatment of Vernet's six "sites" and "Seventh Picture," conducted as a series of conversational promenades with "Monsieur l'abbé," see Diderot, *Salon de 1767*, 159–241 (Goodman, *Diderot on Art*, vol. 2, *The Salon of 1767*, 86–128). On his reading of those promenades, see Michael Fried, *Absorption and Theatricality: Painting and Beholder in the Age of Diderot* (University of California Press, 1980), 122–27. See as well Michael Cartwright, "Diderot's Discursive Eye: Peripatetics and the Search for Harmony," in Undank and Josephs, *Diderot: Digression and Dispersion*, 72–84; and Marian Hobson, *The Object of Art: The Theory of Illusion in Eighteenth-Century France* (Cambridge University Press, 1982).

6. For his six-page discussion of Greuze's *La Jeune fille qui pleure son oiseau mort*, in which he gushes and exclaims over "le joli poème," describing it in detail as he pauses to *vouvoyer* the girl, addressing her directly as his pretty "petite," and offering fatherly comfort to her while imagining the scene with her young lover that led to her deflowering, see Diderot, *Salon de 1765*, 245–51. (For the English translation, see John Goodman, trans., *Diderot on Art*, vol. 1, *The Salon of 1765 and Notes on Painting* [Yale University Press, 1995], 97–100.)

7. For his long discussion of Fragonard's *Le Grand-prêtre Corésus s'immole pour sauver Callirhoé*, see Diderot, *Salon de 1765*, 324–44 (Goodman, *Diderot on Art*, vol. 1, *Salon of 1765*, 141–48): on the first page of the entry, he addresses Grimm directly, telling him that it is "impossible for me to talk to you about this painting" and that instead "I'm going to tell you about a very strange vision which tormented me one night, after a day on which I'd spent the morning looking at the paintings and the evening reading some of Plato's dialogues," before announcing the allegorical device of "Plato's cave" and proceeding to conduct a dialogue with his fictional version of Grimm, which modulates between narrative, description, and oneiric fantasy (Diderot, *Salon de 1767*, 323–24; Goodman, *Diderot on Art*, vol. 1, *Salon of 1765*, 141).

8. The understanding of Diderot's ekphrastic practice as an art critic that is closest to my own is to be found in Louis Marin's "Le descripteur fantaisiste," in *Des Pouvoirs de l'image* (Editions du Seuil, 1993), 72–96, in which he treats Diderot's ekphrastic movement between paintings in the Salon and images "painted" in the imagination by the writer through a close analysis of Diderot's rendering of Francesco Giuseppe Casanova's *Une marche d'armée* in the Salon of 1765, followed by a briefer treatment of the Vernet suite in the Salon of 1767.

9. It was Michael Baxandall whom I remember remarking on what he saw as Diderot's failings as an art critic. See Fried, *Absorption and Theatricality*, in particular chap. 3, "Painting and Beholder," 107–60; and Ewa Lajer-Burcharth, *The Painter's Touch: Boucher, Chardin, Fragonard* (Princeton University Press, 2018): "Diderot sought to translate the unusual effect of [Chardin's] depictions of objects on the viewer . . . by developing a language of vivid description unprecedented in the critical reception of still lifes" (157). See also Thomas Baldwin, "Ekphrasis and Related Issues in Diderot's *Salons*," in *New Essays on Diderot*, ed. James Fowler (Cambridge University Press, 2011), 234–47; and Thomas Baldwin, *The Picture as Spectre in Diderot, Proust, and Deleuze* (Modern Humanities Research Association and Maney Publishing, 2011).

10. See Ruth Webb, *Ekphrasis, Imagination and Persuasion in Ancient Rhetorical Theory and Practice* (Routledge, 2016), especially 1–38. See also James A. W. Heffernan, *Museum of Words: The Poetics of Ekphrasis from Homer to Ashbery* (University of Chicago Press, 1993); and Murray Krieger, *Ekphrasis: The Illusion of the Natural Sign* (Johns Hopkins University Press, 1992).

11. "On Ecphrasis," from "*The* Exercises *of Aelius Theon*" (first century BCE/CE), in *Progymnasmata: Greek Textbooks of Prose Composition and Rhetoric*, trans. George A. Kennedy (Society of Biblical Literature, 2003), 45–47 (my italics).

12. "On Ecphrasis," from "*The* Preliminary Exercises, *Attributed to Hermogenes*" (third–fourth century CE), in Kennedy, *Progymnasmata*, 86.

13. "On Ecphrasis," from "*The* Preliminary Exercises *of Nicolaus the Sophist*" (fifth century CE), in Kennedy, *Progymnasmata*, 166–68.

14. "On Ecphrasis," from the "*Commentary on the* Progymnasmata *of Aphthonius, Attributed to John of Sardis*" (ninth century CE), in Kennedy, *Progymnasmata*, 218–22 (my italics).

15. See Arthur Fairbanks, trans., *Philostratus Imagines/Callistratus Descriptions* (William Heinemann, 1931): "It is a good thing to gather figs and also not to pass over in silence the figs in this picture. Purple figs dripping with juice are heaped on vine-leaves; and they are depicted with breaks in the skin, some just cracking open to disgorge their honey, some split apart, they are so ripe. Near them lies a branch, not bare, by Zeus, or empty of fruit, but under the shade of its leaves are figs, some still green and 'untimely,' some with wrinkled skin and over-ripe, and some about to turn, disclosing the shining juice, while on the tip of the branch a

sparrow buries its bill in what seems the very sweetest of figs. All the ground is strewn with chestnuts, some of which are rubbed free of the burr, others lie quite shut up, and others show the burr breaking at the lines of division. See, too, the pears on pears, apples on apples, both heaps of them and piles of ten, all fragrant and golden. You will say that their redness has not been put on from outside, but has bloomed from within. Here are gifts of the cherry tree, here is fruit in clusters heaped in a basket, and the basket is woven, not from alien twigs, but from branches of the plant itself. And if you look at the vine-sprays woven together and at the clusters hanging from them and how the grapes stand out one by one . . . You would say that even the grapes in the painting are good to eat and full of winey juice. And the most charming point of all this is: on a leafy branch is yellow honey already within the comb and ripe to stream forth if the comb is pressed; and on another leaf is cheese new curdled and quivering; and there are bowls of milk not merely white but gleaming, for the cream floating upon it makes it seem to gleam" (31. Xenia, 123–25). See also Norman Bryson, "Philostratus and the Imaginary Museum," in *Vision and Textuality*, ed. Stephen Melville and Bill Readings (Duke University Press, 1995), 174–94. And on the category of "xenia" (still life), see Norman Bryson, *Looking at the Overlooked: Four Essays on Still Life Painting* (Reaktion Books, 1990); see, in particular, chap. 1, "Xenia," 17–59, in which Bryson discusses two of Philostratus's ekphrases of "xenia," including the one cited above.

16. Denis Diderot, *Salon de 1763*, in Jean Seznec and Jean Adhémar, *Diderot Salons I: 1759/1761/1763* (Clarendon Press, 1957), 222 (my translation and italics). See also Lajer-Burcharth, *Painter's Touch*, 162; and Michael Baxandall, *Shadows and Enlightenment* (Yale University Press, 1995), 111.

17. Diderot, *Salon de 1763*, 223. On the question of technique in Diderot's art criticism, see Florence Boulerie, "Diderot et le vocabulaire technique de l'art," in *Diderot Studies* 30 (2007): 89–113.

18. See Marie-Laure de Rochebrune, "Ceramics and Glass in Chardin's Paintings," in Pierre Rosenberg et al., *Chardin* (Royal Academy Publications; Editions de la Réunion des musées nationaux, 2000), 37–53, for the information about the contents of Chardin's still-life paintings. See also Ewa Lajer-Burcharth, *Chardin Material* (Sternberg Press, 2011); Jean Louis Schefer, *Chardin* (P.O.L., 2002); and René Demoris, *Chardin, la chair et l'objet* (Editions Olbia, 1999).

19. Diderot, *Salon de 1765*, 182 (Goodman, *Diderot on Art*, vol. 1, *Salon of 1765*, 60).

20. Diderot, *Salon de 1765*, 186–87 (Goodman, *Diderot on Art*, vol. 1, *Salon of 1765*, 62–63).

21. Diderot, *Salon de 1765*, 188 (Goodman, *Diderot on Art*, vol. 1, *Salon of 1765*, 63).

22. Diderot, *Salon de 1765*, 189 (Goodman, *Diderot on Art*, vol. 1, *Salon of 1765*, 64). On the question of genre, see Anouchka Vasak, "La Question du genre dans les *Salons*," in *Diderot, l'expérience de l'art*, ed. Geneviève Cammagre and Carole Talon-Hugon (Presses Universitaires de France, 2007), 11–25.

23. Denis Diderot, *Salon de 1759*, in Seznec and Adhémar, *Diderot Salons I*, 30.

24. Edmund de Waal, "Jean-Siméon Chardin, *Still Life with Plums*, ca. 1730," in *The Sleeve Should Be Illegal & Other Reflections on Art at the Frick*, ed. Michaelyn Mitchell (Frick Collection with DelMonico Books, 2021), 39 (my italics). See also Marcel Proust, *Chardin and Rembrandt* (1895), trans. Jennie Feldman (David Zwirner Books, 2017); and Francis Ponge, *De la nature morte et de Chardin* (Hermann, 1963).

25. Wildenstein catalogue (1933), cited in de Rochebrune, "Ceramics and Glass in Chardin's Paintings," 47–48.

26. See Rosenberg, *Chardin*, 292, plate 82.

27. Denis Diderot, "*Art*," in Méricam-Bourdet and Volpilhac-Auger, *Diderot: Articles de l'Encyclopédie*, 82–101, 87.

28. Denis Diderot, "Fayence," *ARTFL Encyclopédie*, vol. 6, 454–60, 455.

29. See Diderot's mention of the *verrerie* essay in his discussion of the making of "Blanc fin," as well as of Kunckel's treatise on "Verrerie" (Antonio Neri, Cristopher Merret, and Johannes Kunckel, *Art de la verrerie* [Durand & Pissot, 1752, derived at least in part from Antonio Neri, *L'Arte Vetraria*, 1612]: Diderot, "Fayence," *ARTFL Encyclopédie*, vol. 6, 458–59). Diderot ends his entry on *fayence* with a reference to the article on porcelain in the *Encyclopedia:* 6:460.

30. Chevalier Louis de Jaucourt, "Verre à boire," *ARTFL Encyclopédie*, vol. 17, 101.

31. For a treatment of painting as a matter of "water and stones," see James Elkins, *What Painting Is: How to Think About Oil Painting, Using the Language of Alchemy* (Routledge, 1999): "Water and stones. Those are the unpromising ingredients of . . . painting, because artists' pigments are made from fluids . . . mixed together with powdered stones to give color. All oil paints, watercolors, gouaches, and acrylics are made that way, and so are more solid concoctions including pastels, ink blocks, crayons, and charcoal. They differ only in proportions of water

and stone—or, to put it more accurately, medium and pigment. To make oil paint, for example, it is only necessary to buy powdered rock and mix it with a medium, say linseed oil, so that it can be spread with a brush. Very little more is involved in any pigment, and the same observations apply to other visual arts. Ceramics begins with the careful mixing of tap water and clay, and the wet clay slip is itself a dense mixture of stone and water. Watery mud is the medium of ceramists, just as oily mud is the medium of painters" (1).

32. For a discussion of the *Encyclopedia*'s illustrations, which rightly treats them as both supporting the humanist rationality of the Encyclopedic project and exceeding that rationality in their surreality, see Roland Barthes, "The Plates of the *Encyclopedia*" (1964), in *New Critical Essays*, trans. Richard Howard (Northwestern University Press, 2009), 23–39. Barthes organizes the plates into "three levels: anthological, since the object, isolated from any context, is presented *in itself;* anecdotic, when it is 'naturalized' by its insertion into a large-scale *tableau vivant* (which is what we call a vignette); genetic, when the image offers us the trajectory from raw substance to finished object: genesis, essence, praxis, the object is thus accounted for in all its categories: sometimes it *is*, sometimes it is *made*, sometimes it even *makes*" (24). Barthes views wood, not glass, as the privileged material of the *Encyclopedia:* "If we visit a World's Fair today, we perceive in all the objects exhibited two or three dominant substances, glass, metal, plastic no doubt; the substance of the Encyclopedic object is of a more vegetal age: it is wood which dominates in this great catalogue; it produces a world of objects easy on the eyes, already human by their substance, resistant but not brittle, constructible but not plastic" (25). In this, Barthes's treatment of the *Encyclopedia*'s plates recalls his own discussion of the materials of wood and plastic in the essays on "Toys" and "Plastic" in *Mythologies* (1957), trans. Annette Lavers (Hill and Wang, 1972), 53–55, 97–99.

33. "Verrerie," *ARTFL Encyclopédie*, vol. 17, 156 (my translation).

34. The purity of optical glass is also stressed: on this question, see Simon Schaffer, "Glassworks: Newton's Prisms and the Uses of Experiment," in *The Uses of Experiment: Studies in the Natural Sciences*, ed. David Gooding, Trevor Pinch, and Simon Schaffer (Cambridge University Press, 1989), 67–104.

35. Jaucourt, "Verre," *ARTFL Encyclopédie*, vol. 17, 92–94 (my translation). On the history of porcelain, see also Edmund de Waal, *The White Road: Journey into an Obsession* (Farrar, Straus & Giroux, 2015).

36. See Jean Baudrillard, "A Model Material: Glass," in chap. 2, "Structures of Atmosphere," *System of Objects* (1968), trans. James Benedict (Verso, 1996), 41–43.

37. On "amorphous solids," see Zbigniew H. Stachurski, *Fundamentals of Amorphous Solids: Structure and Properties* (Wiley-VCH, 2015).

38. On the question of "magic" and "natural philosophy," see Lorraine Daston and Katherine Park, *Wonders and the Order of Nature* (Zone Books, 2001).

39. On Chardin's pictures of children, see Lajer-Burcharth, *Painter's Touch*, 139–53; Juliet Carey, ed., *Taking Time: Chardin's* Boy Building a House of Cards *and Other Paintings* (Rothschild Foundation with Paul Holberton Publishing, 2012); and Dorothy Johnson, "Picturing Pedagogy: Education and the Child in the Paintings of Chardin," *Eighteenth-Century Studies* 24, no. 1 (Fall 1990): 47–68.

40. See Diderot's *Le Rêve d'Alembert*, 1769 (Paris: Flammarion, 2002), for its meditation on the invisible threshold between soul and matter. On that text and others, and their relation to Diderot's theory of matter, see Wilda Anderson, *Diderot's Dream* (Johns Hopkins University Press, 1990). On breath, see also David Abram, "The Commonwealth of Breath," in *Material Ecocriticism*, ed. Serenella Iovino and Serpil Oppermann (Indiana University Press, 2014), 301–14.

2. GIORGIO MORANDI AND THE MATTER OF STILL LIFE

1. On Dutch seventeenth-century painting and its attachment to materialities, see Roland Barthes, "The World as Object" (1954), in *Critical Essays*, trans. Richard Howard (Northwestern University Press, 1972), 3–12. On Dutch Golden Age painting, see as well Joanna Woodall, "Laying the Table: The Procedures of Still Life," *Art History* 35, no. 5 (November 2012): 976–1003; Hanneke Grootenboer, *The Rhetoric of Perspective: Realism and Illusionism in Seventeenth-Century Dutch Still-Life Painting* (University of Chicago Press, 2006); Elizabeth Honig, "Making Sense of Things: On the Motives of Dutch Still Life," *Res: Anthropology and Aesthetics* 34 (September 1998): 166–83; Simon Schama, *The Embarrassment of Riches: An Interpretation of Dutch Culture in the Golden Age* (Vintage Books, 1997); and Svetlana Alpers, *The Art of Describing: Dutch Art in the Seventeenth Century* (University of Chicago Press, 1983).

2. On the question of "material thought," see my own *Cézanne's Gravity* (Yale University Press, 2018).

3. See Hanneke Grootenboer, *The Pensive Image: Art as a Form of Thinking* (University of Chicago Press, 2021); and Viktor Stoichita, *The Self-Aware Image: An Insight into Early Modern Meta-Painting* (Brepols Publishers, 2015).

4. On Giorgio Morandi, see David Leiber, ed., *Giorgio Morandi: Late Paintings* (David Zwirner Books, 2017); Flavio Fergonzi and Elisabetta Barisoni, *Morandi: Master of Modern Still Life* (Phillips Collection, 2009); Maria Cristina Bandera and Renato Miracco, eds., *Morandi, 1890–1964* (Skira, with MAMbo [Museo d'Arte Moderna di Bologna], 2008); Janet Abramowicz, *Giorgio Morandi: The Art of Silence* (Yale University Press, 2005); Donna de Salvo and Matthew Gale, eds., *Giorgio Morandi* (Tate Publishing, 2001); Karen Wilkin, *Giorgio Morandi* (Rizzoli, 1998); *Museo Morandi, Bologna: Il catalogo* (Museo Morandi, 1993); and Lamberto Vitali, *Morandi: Catalogo generale*, 2 vols. (Edizioni Electa, 1983). For the most recent monograph on Morandi, see as well Marilena Pasquali, *Giorgio Morandi: Time Suspended* (Skira, 2024).

5. The British artist Tacita Dean would make two 2009 films in Morandi's studio, one of which, *Still Life*, panned over that "ground plan." See Massimo Minnini and Augusto Morari, *Giorgio Morandi e Tacita Dean: "Semplice come tutta la mia vita"* (Centro Internazionale d'Arte e di Cultura di Palazzo Te, with Skira, 2017).

6. See Joel Meyerowitz, *Morandi's Objects* (Damiani, 2015).

7. On Morandi's studio, see Lorenzo de Bianchi, *Giorgio Morandi's Studio: Photographs by Gianni Berengo Gardin* (Charta, 2009). See as well Arnaldo Beccaria, *L'ultimo visita a Giorgio Morandi* (Edizioni Ogni uomo è tutt gli uomini, 2017); and Neri Pozza, *I modelli di Giorgio Morandi* (Edizioni Ogni uomo è tutt gli uomini, 2016). On his gessoing and painting of his bottles and other vessels, see Matthew Gale, "white bottle—red earth," in de Salvo and Gale, *Giorgio Morandi*, 86–101.

8. On "rhopography," see Norman Bryson, *Looking at the Overlooked: Four Essays on Still Life Painting* (Reaktion Books, 1990), in particular 60–95.

9. For a comparison of the serial procedures of Morandi and Albers, see Elizabeth Gordon, ed., *Albers and Morandi: Never Finished* (David Zwirner Books, 2021).

10. See Clement Greenberg, "Toward a Newer Laocoön" (1939), in *Clement Greenberg: The Collected Essays and Criticism*, vol. 1, *Perceptions and Judgments, 1939–1944*, ed. John O'Brian (University of Chicago Press, 1986), 23–38.

11. On this aspect of Cézanne's work, see "The Landscape of Still Life," in my *Cézanne in the Studio: Still Life in Watercolors* (J. Paul Getty Museum with Oxford University Press, 2004), 45–73. My view of the strange lack of eroticism in Cézanne's nudes would seem to run against Aruna D'Souza's argument in her *Cézanne's Bathers: Biography and the Erotics of Paint* (Pennsylvania State University Press, 2008); in fact, I do not disagree with her understanding of the displacement of erotic charge, in Cézanne's paintings of the nude, from the depicted body into the facture used to render it.

12. Many are the instances in which artists and other writers speak to the landscape, architectural, and figural resonances of Morandi's arrays of simple objects. For one particularly eloquent example, see Wayne Thiebaud, "A Fellow Painter's View of Giorgio Morandi," in Leiber, *Giorgio Morandi: Late Paintings*, 74–75, on Morandi's "ineffable microworlds": "Tableaus and friezes in scene after scene infer arresting little dramas. Elegant tall bottles portray royal Venetian courtesans in an attitude of stately imperiousness. Dark worlds, ominous Machiavellian intrigues, may be suggested. Sometimes shadowy forms describe an ambiguous underworld. Yet in another picture the bright fresh light of Bologna sets a morning scene. There are fat clay clowns, wooden soldiers, China virgins, pompous cardinals, copper freaks, and caricatures of many kinds." For another, see Alexi Worth, "Flat Light," also in Leiber, *Giorgio Morandi: Late Paintings*, 76–78: "horizontal foils to the mostly vertical architecture . . . / . . . his cherished objects assembled like children in a family photo . . . / . . . Now the objects become still shoulder-to-shoulder icons: Bowl. Vase. Cloth. Box. Vase . . . / . . . This may sound absurd in a world of crockery, a world so apparently inanimate. But it's not exactly clear that Morandi's world—with its trembling, fluttering, anti-mechanical contours—is inanimate after all." See also Wilkin, *Giorgio Morandi*, 99: "the same objects are treated like an urban crowd in a piazza. In still others, objects are pressed and staggered like the buildings of a town on the fertile Emilian plains . . . / Just as we become familiar with Cézanne's cast of characters . . . we easily come to recognize Morandi's protagonists." Abramowicz put it this way, in *Giorgio Morandi: The Art of Silence*, speaking of the Bolognese aspect of Morandi's still lifes: "City architecture has affected few modern artists as much as the urban landscape of Bologna influenced Morandi, and it became subject matter to be transformed into his still lifes" (17).

13. It was Georges Braque who commented that still life opened onto "a tactile space, I would say almost a manual space" ("une espace tactile, je dirais presque manuel")—as quoted in Dora Vallier, "Braque, la peinture et nous: Propos de l'artiste," *Cahiers d'Art* 29, no. 1 (October 1954): 16.

14. On the question of the "indexical" sign, see C. S. Peirce, "Logic as Semiotic: The Theory of Signs," *Philosophic Writings of Peirce* (Dover Publications, 1955), especially 106; and Rosalind Krauss, "Notes on the Index: Parts 1 and 2," *The Originality of the Avant-Garde and Other Modernist Myths* (MIT Press, 1985), 196–219.

15. Morandi's remark, translated as "There is nothing more abstract than reality," is repeated over and over again by everyone writing about him. See, for example, David Leiber, foreword to *Giorgio Morandi: Late Paintings*, 8; and Wilkin, *Giorgio Morandi*, 122 (for a longer variation on that comment). It is also the title of Renato Miracco's essay in the 2008 MAMbo catalogue, Bandero and Miracco, *Morandi, 1890–1964*, 290–305: "Nothing Is More Abstract Than Reality." See also Karen Wilkin et al., *Giorgio Morandi: Works, Writings, Interviews* (Ediciones Poligrafa, 2025).

16. Calling Morandi "a poet of matter," Umberto Eco said it this way: "Morandi is not a painter 'of matter' like those I have just mentioned but presents a link between figurative painting and painting 'of matter.' Beneath the seemingly repetitive nature of an unvarying figurative discourse, Morandi spent his entire life addressing the problem of the redemption of matter." Umberto Eco, "My First Morandi," in Bandero and Miracco, *Morandi, 1890–1964*, 343–44.

17. Most writers now seem to agree that Morandi was *both* a traditionalist *and* a modernist; in his own time, he was criticized, alternately, for both aspects of his work. For the questions of Italian tradition, the valuing of figure painting and the devaluing of still life, and Morandi's fractious relation to the Accademia di Belle Arti where he trained and then became a professor of etching, see Abramowicz, *Giorgio Morandi: The Art of Silence*, 23–35.

18. Wilkin remarks that Morandi "clearly preferred Giotto, Uccello, Piero, and Masaccio" and that among them, "Giotto is arguably the most important." Wilkin, *Giorgio Morandi*, 68, 72. Morandi himself wrote, "Among the ancient painters, the Tuscans are those most interest me—Giotto and Masaccio above all. As for their modern counterparts, I regard Corot, Courbet, Fattori, and Cézanne as the most legitimate heirs to the glorious Italian tradition." Morandi, "Autobiography," in Bandero and Miracco, *Morandi, 1890–1964*, 346–47. See also Neville

Rowley, "A 'Light Without Color': Giorgio Morandi and Piero della Francesca," in Bandero and Miracco, *Morandi, 1890–1964*, 106–17.

19. On Morandi's interest in Caravaggio, see Wilkin, *Giorgio Morandi*, 53; Wilkin also lists "Seurat, Chardin, Corot, Cézanne, Georges de la Tour, Giotto, and Piero della Francesca" as artists represented in Morandi's library of "handsome volumes."

20. On this and other Italian still lifes, see Charles Sterling, *Still-Life Painting from Antiquity to the Present* (Harper & Row, 1981), 80–92; and Mina Gregori, *The Italian Still Life: From Caravaggio to the 18th Century* (Electa, 2004).

21. On different kinds of shadow-casting, see Michael Baxandall, *Shadows and Enlightenment* (Yale University Press, 1995), in particular 119–44.

22. On this painting, and its relatives, see Bryson, "Rhopography," *Looking at the Overlooked*, 60–95. See also Kenneth Bendiner, *Food in Painting: From the Renaissance to the Present* (Reaktion Books, 2004), 89. See as well Sterling, *Still-Life Painting*, 92–101, and my own self-published *Still Lives* (Blurb, 2012), from which several of these excursuses are derived.

23. On the painter's pigments, and the shift from valuing paintings according to their materials to valuing them according to the painter's illusionistic skills, see Michael Baxandall, *Painting and Experience in Fifteenth-Century Italy: A Primer in the Social History of Style* (Oxford University Press, 1986), 1–28. See as well James Elkins, *What Painting Is* (Routledge, 1999), in particular 1–39.

24. On the nautilus cup, see Marisa Anne Bass, *Conchophilia: Shells, Art and Curiosity in Early Modern Europe* (Princeton University Press, 2023), in particular Claudia Swan, "The Nature of Exotic Shells," 21–47, and Anna Grasskamp, "Shells, Bodies, and the Collector's Cabinet," 48–71. (It is also worth noting that very occasionally Morandi included conch and scallop shells in his compositions.)

25. On the question of trade as the underpinnings of Dutch still life, see Julie Berger Hochstrasser, *Still Life and Trade in the Dutch Golden Age* (Yale University Press, 2007). See also Bryson, "Abundance," *Looking at the Overlooked*, 96–135 (which begins its discussion of Dutch seventeenth-century still-life painting with a gesture to one of Morandi's still lifes).

26. On Gijsbrechts, see Olaf Koester et al., *Painted Illusions: The Art of Cornelius Gijsbrechts* (National Gallery, 2000).

27. See Claude Lévi-Strauss, *The Raw and the Cooked*, vol. 1 of *Mythologiques*, trans. John and Doreen Weightman (University of Chicago Press, 1983).

28. On Chardin's still lifes, see the first essay in this volume, my "Chardin, Diderot and the Muteness of Made Things: Between Ekphrasis and the Encyclopedia." See as well Ewa Lajer-Burcharth, *The Painter's Touch: Boucher, Chardin, Fragonard* (Princeton University Press, 2018), 86–175.

29. As Wilkin puts it (*Giorgio Morandi*, 102), "it is easy to understand why Morandi has been compared so often with Chardin." (One specific example of that affinity is Morandi's 1920 vase of flowers, which echoes the one floral still life that Chardin painted.)

30. On this painting in particular, and more generally on the topic of the relation between painting and food, see Bendiner, *Food in Painting*, especially 75–108; and Marni Reva Kessler, *Discomfort Food: The Culinary Imagination in Late Nineteenth-Century French Art* (University of Minnesota Press, 2021). See also my *Manet Manette* (Yale University Press, 2002), 269–85.

31. This anecdote was incorporated into Marcel Proust's *In Search of Lost Time*, in vol. 3, *The Guermantes Way*, trans. C. K. Scott Moncrieff and Terence Kilmartin (Chatto & Windus, 1992), 577–78. See Eric Karpeles, *Paintings in Proust: A Visual Companion to* In Search of Lost Time (Thames & Hudson, 2017), 18, 176.

32. On the commodity and its embodying of the abstraction of exchange value, see Karl Marx, "The Commodity" (1867), in *Capital: A Critique of Political Economy*, vol. 1, trans. Ben Fowkes (Penguin Classics, 1990), 125–77.

33. Tom Lubbock, "Fantin-Latour, Henri: White Cup and Saucer (1864)," *The Independent*, March 7, 2008, https://www.independent.co.uk/arts-entertainment/art/great-works/fantinlatour-henri-white-cup-and-saucer-1864-792581.html. In addition to his more famous floral compositions, Fantin-Latour painted other simple still lifes featuring single or double objects, such as his *Still Life with Teacup* (1859), *Still Life with Cup and Clay Pot* and *Still Life with Mustard Pot* (both 1860), *Still Life with Inkwell* (1861), *Plate of Peaches* (1862), *Candlestick* (1870), and *Strawberries on a Small Earthenware Plate* (1872), among others.

34. Ali Smith, "Elegy in a Cup and Saucer," Fitzwilliam Museum, https://fitzmuseum.cam.ac.uk/conversations/podcasts/in-my-minds-eye/elegy-in-a-cup-and-saucer-ali-smith, 2023.

35. A. S. Byatt, "As Seen by A. S. Byatt," Fitzwilliam Museum. 2008. April 14, 2010 http://www.fitzmuseum.cam.uk/gallery/inspirations/contribution/byatt.html, 2008. On this piece and other passages on paintings in Byatt's work, see Elizabeth Hicks, "Public and Private Collections in A. S. Byatt's 'The Children's Book,'" *Mosaic: An Interdisciplinary Critical Journal* 44, no. 2 (June 2011): 171–85.

36. See Edmund de Waal, *The White Road: Journey into an Obsession* (Farrar, Straus & Giroux, 2015). See also Edmund de Waal, "Witness," in *Giorgio Morandi: Time Suspended*, ed. Marilena Pasquali (Skira, 2024), 45–53, in which he speaks of the way his own focus on white porcelain bottles should "be on nodding terms with him [Morandi]" (51).

37. On Morandi and Cézanne, see Wilkin, *Giorgio Morandi*, 60, 72, 109.

38. On this painting, see my *Cézanne's Gravity*, 1–21.

39. On this and others of Cézanne's watercolored still lifes, see my *Cézanne in the Studio*, in particular p. 33.

40. On Ben Nicholson, see Lee Beard, Louise Campbell, Simon Martin, Edmund de Waal, and Louise Weller, *Ben Nicholson: From the Studio* (Pallant House Gallery, 2021), 10 (quoted from Laura Mattioli Rossi, *The Later Morandi: Still Lifes 1950–1964* [Mazotta, 1998], 61). In that context, Edmund de Waal writes sensitively about Ben Nicholson's still lifes ("Ben Nicholson," 16–22), at one point quoting Morandi thus: "'A white bottle is all that remains,' writes Morandi" (19). It is worth remarking that Nicholson had his own white "English pottery bottle"; indeed, he was photographed with it in 1935. It is also worth remarking that an exhibition bringing the art of Ben Nicholson together with that of Morandi and de Waal was held in the Crane Kalman Gallery in London in 2011: *Still Lives: Giorgio Morandi, Edmund de Waal, Ben Nicholson*. See also Paul Coldwell, *Morandi's Legacy: Influences on British Art* (Philip Wilson Publishers, 2006). On William Nicholson, see Colin Campbell, Merlin James, Patricia Reed and Sanford Schwartz, *The Art of William Nicholson* (Royal Academy of Arts, 2005).

41. On the objects in Ben Nicholson's studio, his "white reliefs," and his marriage to the sculptor Barbara Hepworth, see Louise Weller, "Ben Nicholson: From the Studio"; Lee Beard, "Making and Meaning: Ideas and Process in the Work of Ben Nicholson"; and Louise Campbell, "'Architecture and the Painter': The Studios of Ben Nicholson," in Lee Beard et al., *Ben Nicholson: From the Studio*, 34–118. In addition to his numerous other travels to and stays in Italy, Ben

Nicholson represented Britain in the 1954 Venice Biennale, together with Francis Bacon and Lucian Freud (Beard et al., *Ben Nicholson: From the Studio*, 122).

42. See D. W. Winnicott, *Playing and Reality* (Routledge Classics, 2005), especially chaps. 3 and 4, "Playing: A Theoretical Statement" and "Playing: Creative Activity and the Search for the Self," 51–86; for the "third area" or "potential space" of play, see in particular 72, 135: "The place where cultural experience is located is in the *potential space* between the individual and the environment (originally the object). The same can be said of playing . . . / . . . *in the potential space between the subjective object and the object objectively perceived*, between me-extensions and the not-me."

43. On Cézanne's remark that the painter "thinks in painting" (quoted by Maurice Merleau-Ponty in his essay "Eye and Mind," in *Merleau-Ponty: Basic Writings*, ed. Thomas Baldwin [Routledge, 2004], 309), see my *Cézanne's Gravity*, 93.

44. On Morandi's service in World War I, his breakdown, and his vexed involvements with first Futurism and then Fascism, see Abramowicz, *Giorgio Morandi: The Art of Silence*, especially 37–49. On object-relations theory, see Jay Greenberg and Stephen Mitchell, *Object Relations in Psychoanalytic Theory* (Harvard University Press, 1983).

45. See Abramowicz, who had been a student of Morandi's at the Bologna Accademia de Belle Arti, on his mythologizing of his reputation as a shut-in: *Giorgio Morandi: The Art of Silence*, in particular 193–231. In fact, Morandi appears to have been a sociable man, who exhibited widely (both in Italy—including at the Venice Biennale—and abroad) and traveled occasionally, though almost entirely within Italy.

46. On Morandi and the "Scuola Metafisica," see Wilkin, *Giorgio Morandi*, 80–90; and Abramowicz, *Giorgio Morandi: The Art of Silence*, 51–77.

47. On Morandi's etchings, see Janet Abramowicz, "A World in Black and White: The Imagery and Technique of Morandi's Etchings," in Bandero and Miracco, *Morandi, 1890–1964*, 118–29; and Jennifer Mundy and Christopher Le Brun, *Giorgio Morandi: Etchings* (Tate Gallery Publications, 1992). For Morandi's sensitive watercolors as well as his etchings, see also Ernst Gerhard Guese and Franz A. Morat, *Morandi: Paintings, Watercolors, Drawings, Etchings* (Prestel, 1999).

48. Winnicott insisted that the objects that the child plays with—and by extension the objects that are created in and by adult culture—are both found

and made; at the same time, he insisted that the paradox of the "third" or "intermediate area"—that it is a space at once internal and external to the self, at once an illusion and a reality—remain held in suspension: see Winnicott, *Playing and Reality*, 17–19 in particular. There is much that Winnicott's theory shares with Walter Benjamin's late-1920s essays on toys and play, as well as with Johan Huizinga's *Homo Ludens* (1938) and Roger Caillois's *Les jeux et les hommes* (1958), but his was the theory that played out in therapeutic practice—that is to say, in which imaginative play actually took place physically and experientially, happening in a shared external world.

BIBLIOGRAPHY

Abramowicz, Janet. *Giorgio Morandi: The Art of Silence*. Yale University Press, 2005.

Agin, Shane. "The Development of Diderot's Salons and the Shifting Boundary of Representational Language." *Diderot Studies* 30 (2007): 11–29.

Alpers, Svetlana. *The Art of Describing: Dutch Art in the Seventeenth Century*. University of Chicago Press, 1983.

Anderson, Wilda. *Diderot's Dream*. Johns Hopkins University Press, 1990.

Armstrong, Carol. *Cézanne in the Studio: Still Life in Watercolors*. J. Paul Getty Museum, 2004.

Armstrong, Carol. *Cézanne's Gravity*. Yale University Press, 2018.

Armstrong, Carol. *Manet Manette*. Yale University Press, 2002.

Armstrong, Carol. *Still Lives*. Blurb, 2012.

Baldwin, Thomas, ed. *Merleau-Ponty: Basic Writings*. Routledge, 2004.

Baldwin, Thomas. *The Picture as Spectre in Diderot, Proust, and Deleuze*. Modern Humanities Research Association and Maney Publishing, 2011.

Bandera, Maria Cristina, and Renato Miracco, eds. *Morandi, 1890–1964*. Skira, with Museo d'Arte Moderna di Bologna, 2008.

Barthes, Roland. *Critical Essays*. Translated by Richard Howard. Northwestern University Press, 1972.

Barthes, Roland. *Mythologies*. Translated by Annette Lavers. Hill and Wang, 1972.

Barthes, Roland. *New Critical Essays*. Translated by Richard Howard. Northwestern University Press, 2009.

Bass, Marisa Anne, ed. *Conchophilia: Shells, Art and Curiosity in Early Modern Europe.* Princeton University Press, 2023.

Baudrillard, Jean. *The System of Objects.* Translated by James Benedict. Verso, 1996.

Baxandall, Michael. *Painting and Experience in Fifteenth-Century Italy: A Primer in the Social History of Pictorial Style.* Oxford University Press, 1982.

Baxandall, Michael. *Shadows and Enlightenment.* Yale University Press, 1995.

Beard, Lee, Louise Campbell, Simon Martin, Edmund de Waal, and Louise Weller. *Ben Nicholson: From the Studio.* Pallant House Gallery, 2021.

Beccaria, Arnaldo. *L'ultimo visita a Giorgio Morandi.* Edizioni Ogni uomo è tutt gli uomini, 2017.

Belleguic, Thierry, ed. *Diderot Studies* 30. Librairie Droz, 2007.

Bendiner, Kenneth. *Food in Painting: From the Renaissance to the Present.* Reaktion Books, 2004.

Bennett, Jane. *Vibrant Matter: A Political Ecology of Things.* Duke University Press, 2010.

Bertucci, Paola. *Artisanal Enlightenment: Science and the Mechanical Arts in Old Regime France.* Yale University Press, 2017.

Brewer, Daniel, and Julie Candler Hayes, eds. *Using the* Encyclopédie*: Ways of Knowing, Ways of Reading.* Voltaire Foundation, 2002.

Brown, Bill, ed. *Things.* A Critical Inquiry Book. University of Chicago Press, 2004.

Bryson, Norman. *Looking at the Overlooked: Four Essays on Still Life Painting.* Reaktion Books, 1990.

Bukdahl, Else Marie. *Diderot critique d'art,* 2 vols. Rosenkilde et Bagger, 1980.

Bukdahl, Else Marie, Michel Delon, Didier Kahn, and Annette Lorenceau, eds. *Diderot: Salons IV: Héros et martyrs: Salons de 1769, 1771, 1775, 1781.* Hermann, 1995.

Byatt, A.S. "As Seen by A.S. Byatt." Fitzwilliam Museum, April 14, 2010. http://www.fitzmuseum.cam.uk/gallery/inspirations/contribution/byatt.html.

Cammagre, Geneviève, and Carole Talon-Hugon. *Diderot, l'expérience de l'art.* Presses Universitaires de France, 2007.

Campbell, Colin, Merlin James, Patricia Reed, and Sanford Schwartz. *The Art of William Nicholson.* Royal Academy of Arts, 2005.

Carey, Juliet, ed. *Taking Time: Chardin's* Boy Building a House of Cards *and Other Paintings.* Rothschild Foundation with Paul Holberton Publishing, 2012.

Coldwell, Paul. *Morandi's Legacy: Influences on British Art*. Philip Wilson Publishers, 2006.

Daston, Lorraine, and Katherine Park. *Wonders and the Order of Nature*. Zone Books, 2001.

De Bianchi, Lorenzo. *Giorgio Morandi's Studio: Photographs by Gianni Berengo Gardin*. Charta, 2009.

De Salvo, Donna, and Matthew Gale, eds. *Giorgio Morandi*. Tate Publishing, 2001.

De Waal, Edmund. *The White Road: Journey into an Obsession*. Farrar, Straus & Giroux, 2015.

Déan, Philippe. *Diderot devant l'image*. Harmattan, 2000.

Delon, Michel. "Les Essais sur la peinture ou la place de la théorie." *Diderot Studies* 30 (2007): 31–51.

Demoris, René. *Chardin, la chair et l'objet*. Editions Olbia, 1999.

Diderot, Denis. *Le Rêve d'Alembert*. Flammarion, 2002.

Diderot, Denis. *Oeuvres de Diderot: Salons*. Vol. 1. J. L. J. Brière, 1821.

Diderot, Denis, and Jean le Rond d'Alembert, eds., *Encyclopédie, ou dictionnaire raisonné des sciences, des arts et des métiers, etc*. University of Chicago: ARTFL Encyclopédie Project, Spring 2021 Edition, Robert Morrissey and Glenn Roe, eds., http://encyclopedie.uchicago.edu/.

D'Souza, Aruna. *Cézanne's Bathers: Biography and the Erotics of Paint*. Pennsylvania State University Press, 2008.

Elkins, James. *What Painting Is: How to Think About Oil Painting, Using the Language of Alchemy*. Routledge, 1999.

Fairbanks, Arthur, trans. *Philostratus Imagines/Callistratus Descriptions*. William Heinemann, 1931.

Fergonzi, Flavio, and Elisabetta Barisoni. *Morandi: Master of Modern Still Life*. Phillips Collection, 2009.

Fowler, James, ed. *New Essays on Diderot*. Cambridge University Press, 2011.

Fried, Michael. *Absorption and Theatricality: Painting and Beholder in the Age of Diderot*. University of California Press, 1980.

Garfield, Simon. *All the Knowledge in the World: The Extraordinary History of the Encyclopedia*. Harper Collins, 2022.

Gooding, Trevor Pinch, and Simon Schaffer, eds. *The Uses of Experiment: Studies in the Natural Sciences*. Cambridge University Press, 1989.

Goodman, John, ed. & trans. *Diderot on Art*. Vols. 1 and 2, *The Salon of 1765* and *The Salon of 1767*. Yale University Press, 1995.

Gordon, Elizabeth, ed. *Albers and Morandi: Never Finished*. David Zwirner Books, 2021.

Greenberg, Jay, and Stephen Mitchell. *Object Relations in Psychoanalytic Theory*. Harvard University Press, 1983.

Gregori, Mina. *The Italian Still Life: From Caravaggio to the 18th Century*. Electa, 2004.

Grootenboer, Hanneke. *The Pensive Image: Art as a Form of Thinking*. University of Chicago Press, 2021.

Grootenboer, Hanneke. *The Rhetoric of Perspective: Realism and Illusionism in Seventeenth-Century Dutch Still-Life Painting*. University of Chicago Press, 2006.

Guese, Ernst Gerhard, and Franz A. Morat. *Morandi: Paintings, Watercolors, Drawings, Etchings*. Prestel, 1999.

Heffernan, James A. W. *Museum of Words: The Poetics of Ekphrasis from Homer to Ashbery*. University of Chicago Press, 1993.

Hicks, Elizabeth. "Public and Private Collections in A. S. Byatt's 'The Children's Book.'" *Mosaic: An Interdisciplinary Critical Journal* 44, no. 2 (2011): 171–85.

Hobson, Marian. *The Object of Art: The Theory of Illusion in Eighteenth-Century France*. Cambridge University Press, 1982.

Hochstrasser, Julie Berger. *Still Life and Trade in the Dutch Golden Age*. Yale University Press, 2007.

Hollander, John, ed. *The Gazer's Spirit: Poems Speaking to Silent Works of Art*. University of Chicago Press, 1995.

Honig, Elizabeth. "Making Sense of Things: On the Motives of Dutch Still Life." *Res: Anthropology and Aesthetics* 34 (1998): 166–83.

Ingold, Tim. *Making: Anthropology, Archaeology, Art and Architecture*. Routledge, 2013.

Iovino, Serenella, and Serpil Oppermann, eds. *Material Ecocriticism*. Indiana University Press, 2014.

Johnson, Dorothy. "Picturing Pedagogy: Education and the Child in the Paintings of Chardin." *Eighteenth-Century Studies* 24, no. 1 (Fall 1990): 47–68.

Karpeles, Eric. *Paintings in Proust: A Visual Companion to* In Search of Lost Time. Thames & Hudson, 2017.

Kennedy, George A., ed. and trans. *Progymnasmata: Greek Textbooks of Prose Composition and Rhetoric*. Society of Biblical Literature, 2003.

Kessler, Marni. *Discomfort Food: The Culinary Imagination in Late Nineteenth-Century French Art*. University of Minnesota Press, 2021.

Koester, Olaf, et al. *Painted Illusions: The Art of Cornelius Gijsbrechts*. National Gallery, 2000.

Krauss, Rosalind. *The Originality of the Avant-Garde and Other Modernist Myths*. MIT Press, 1985.

Krieger, Murray. *Ekphrasis: The Illusion of the Natural Sign*. Johns Hopkins University Press, 1992.

Lajer-Burcharth, Ewa. *Chardin Material*. Sternberg Press, 2011.

Lajer-Burcharth, Ewa. *The Painter's Touch: Boucher, Chardin, Fragonard*. Princeton University Press, 2018.

Lange-Berndt, Petra, ed. *Materiality*. Whitechapel Gallery, 2015.

Leiber, David, ed. *Giorgio Morandi: Late Paintings*. David Zwirner Books, 2017.

Lévi-Strauss, Claude. *The Raw and the Cooked*. Vol. 1 of *Mythologiques*. Translated by John and Doreen Weightman. University of Chicago Press, 1983.

Lough, John. *Inventory of Diderot's Encyclopédie: Plates*. Liverpool University Press with the Voltaire Foundation, 1984.

Lubbock, Tom. "Chardin, Jean-Baptiste Siméon: Glass of Water and Coffee Pot (1760)." *The Independent*, February 17, 2006. https://www.independent.co.uk/arts-entertainment/art/great-works/chardin-jeanbaptiste-simeon-glass-of-water-and-coffee-pot-1760-798010.html.

Lubbock, Tom. "Fantin-Latour, Henri: White Cup and Saucer (1864)." *The Independent*, March 7, 2008. https://www.independent.co.uk/arts-entertainment/art/great-works/fantinlatour-henri-white-cup-and-saucer-1864-792581.html.

Marin, Louis. *Des Pouvoirs de l'image*. Editions du Seuil, 1993.

Marx, Karl. *Capital: A Critique of Political Economy, Volume One*. Translated by Ben Fowkes. Penguin Classics, 1990.

Melville, Stephen, and Bill Readings, eds. *Vision and Textuality*. Duke University Press, 1995.

Méricam-Bourdet, Myrtille, and Catherine Volpilhac, eds. *Diderot: Articles de l'Encyclopédie*. Gallimard, 2015.

Meyerowitz, Joel. *Morandi's Objects*. Damiani, 2015.

Minnini, Massimo, and Augusto Morari. *Giorgio Morandi e Tacita Dean: "Semplice come tutta la mia vita."* Centro Internazionale d'Arte e di Cultura di Palazzo Te, with Skira, 2017.

Mitchell, Michaelyn, ed. *The Sleeve Should Be Illegal & Other Reflections on Art at the Frick*. Frick Collection with DelMonico Books, 2021.

Morley, John. *Diderot and the Encyclopaedists*. Chapman and Hall, 1884.

Mundy, Jennifer, and Christopher Le Brun. *Giorgio Morandi: Etchings*. Tate Gallery Publications, 1992.

Museo Morandi, Bologna: Il catalogo. Museo Morandi, 1993.

O'Brian, John, ed. *Clement Greenberg: The Collected Essays and Criticism*. Vol. 1, *Perceptions and Judgments, 1939–1944*. University of Chicago Press, 1986.

Pasquali, Marilena, ed. *Giorgio Morandi: Time Suspended*. Skira, 2024.

Payen, Jacques, and Roger Lewinter, eds. *Diderot Encyclopedia: The Complete Illustrations 1762–1777*. 4 volumes and index. Harry N. Abrams, 1978.

Peirce, C. S. *Philosophic Writings of Peirce*. Dover Publications, 1955.

Ponge, Francis. *De la nature morte et de Chardin*. Hermann, 1963.

Pozza, Neri. *I modelli di Giorgio Morandi*. Edizioni Ogni uomo è tutt gli uomini, 2016.

Proust, Jacques. *Diderot et l'Encyclopédie*. Armand Colin, 1967.

Proust, Marcel. *Chardin and Rembrandt*. Translated by Jennie Feldman. 1895; David Zwirner Books, 2017.

Roberts, Jennifer L. "Things: Material Turn, Transnational Turn." *American Art* 31, no. 2 (2019): 64–69.

Rosenberg, Pierre, et al. *Chardin*. Royal Academy Publications/Editions de la Réunion des musées nationaux, 2000.

Rossi, Laura Mattioli. *The Later Morandi: Still Lifes 1950–1964*. Mazotta, 1998.

Schama, Simon. *The Embarrassment of Riches: An Interpretation of Dutch Culture in the Golden Age*. Vintage Books, 1997.

Schefer, Jean Louis. *Chardin*. P.O.L., 2002.

Seznec, Jean, and Jean Adhémar. *Diderot Salons I: 1759/1761/1763*. Clarendon Press, 1957.

Smith, Ali. "Elegy in a Cup and Saucer," 2023. Fitzwilliam Museum. https://fitzmuseum.cam.ac.uk/conversations/podcasts/in-myminds-eye/elegy-in-a-cup-and-saucer-ali-smith.

Stachurski, Zbigniew H. *Fundamentals of Amorphous Solids: Structure and Properties*. Wiley-VCH, 2015.

Starobinski, Jean. *Diderot dans l'espace des peintres*. Réunion des Musées Nationaux, 1992.

Sterling, Charles. *Still-Life Painting from Antiquity to the Present*. Harper & Row, 1981.

Stoichita, Viktor. *The Self-Aware Image: An Insight into Early Modern Meta-Painting*. Brepols Publishers, 2015.

Undank, Jack, and Herbert Josephs, eds. *Diderot: Digression and Dispersion, A Bicentennial Tribute*. French Forum Publishers, 1984.

Vallier, Dora. "Braque, la peinture et nous: Propos de l'artiste." *Cahiers d'Art* 29, no. 1 (October 1954): 16.

Vitali, Lamberto. *Morandi: catalogo generale*, 2 vols. Edizioni Electa, 1983.

Webb, Ruth. *Ekphrasis, Imagination and Persuasion in Ancient Rhetorical Theory and Practice*. Routledge, 2016.

Wilkin, Karen. *Giorgio Morandi*. Rizzoli, 1998.

Wilkin, Karen, Peppino Mangravite, and Edouard Roditi. *Giorgio Morandi: Works, Writings, Interviews*. Ediciones Poligrafa, 2025.

Winnicott, D. W. *Playing and Reality*. Routledge Classics, 2005.

Woodall, Joanna. "Laying the Table: The Procedures of Still Life," *Art History* 35, no. 5 (2012): 976–1003.

ILLUSTRATIONS

INDEX

Page numbers in italics refer to figures.

Founded in 1893,
UNIVERSITY OF CALIFORNIA PRESS
publishes bold, progressive books and journals on topics in the arts, humanities, social sciences, and natural sciences—with a focus on social justice issues—that inspire thought and action among readers worldwide.

The UC PRESS FOUNDATION
raises funds to uphold the press's vital role as an independent, nonprofit publisher, and receives philanthropic support from a wide range of individuals and institutions—and from committed readers like you. To learn more, visit ucpress.edu/supportus.